Natur

COOKING WORKBOOK

Other books by Ernestine Finley

NATURAL LIFESTYLE COOKING

Natural Lifestyle
COOKING WORKBOOK

ERNESTINE FINLEY, BS, BA

Pacific Press®
Publishing Association

Nampa, Idaho | Oshawa, Ontario, Canada
www.pacificpress.com

Cover design by Pacific Press®
Cover design resources from Ernestine Finley
Photography by David Johns
Inside design by Kristin Hansen-Mellish

Copyright © 2013 by Pacific Press® Publishing Association
Printed in the United States of America
All rights reserved.

Unless otherwise noted, Scripture quotations are from The New King James Version, copyright © 1979, 1980, 1982, Thomas Nelson, Inc., Publishers.

You can obtain additional copies of this book by calling toll-free 1-800-765-6955
or by visiting http://www.adventistbookcenter.com.

ISBN 13: 978-0-8163-4517-5
ISBN 10: 0-8163-4517-1

13 14 15 16 17 • 5 4 3 2 1

Acknowledgments

The production of a cooking school workbook is a huge task. Each recipe must be checked and rechecked. The food must be purchased and then prepared. Pictures of the food displays must be taken. And of course in any project like this there is a lot of clean up that has to be done. When it comes to writing the workbook, the original manuscript must be edited and all the scientific data must be verified. It takes a dedicated team to care for all these details. I would like to express special thanks to the following people who helped me fix food, set up for photos, photograph various pictures, and clean up. I would also like to express thanks to the editors and designers as well as my family, who supported me through the project.

My husband Mark. Thank you for working with me through the years in many of the cooking schools. It has certainly been fun for me and enriched the classes. Thank you also for the tireless hours you spent reviewing the class material and strengthening it.

My children—Debbie Boland, DO; Rebecca Barnhurst, RD; Mark Jr., PA-C. I want to thank each of you for the support you have given me. I am thankful that all of you have chosen service-oriented careers in the medical field. Your service and dedication to people has inspired me.

David Johns. A very special thanks to you. After all the work of photographing the pictures for the *Natural Lifestyle Cooking* cookbook, I really appreciate your taking on the enormous job of photographing food and various pictures to illustrate this workbook as well.

Nancy Hansen Orr. Thank you for assisting me again in so many areas. Shopping, preparing recipes, and helping me set up food displays. Thank you especially for giving me the encouragement to keep going when I was exhausted after a long day's work.

Joanne Hansen and the Orr family. Thank you again for the enjoyable hours we spent at your home photographing all the pictures so the workbook could be illustrated well.

Colleen Anderson, Judi Johns, Kelly Plank, Amanda Plank, Anna Plank, and Sue Walden. Thank you for your unselfish service of making recipes, loaning props and dishes, and cleaning up. I would like to give an extra special thanks to Sue, who helped not only make various recipes, clean up, but also cook many meals for my family so I could work on this project.

Pacific Press®—Dale Galusha, Bonnie Tyson-Flyn, Kristin Hansen-Mellish, and Jerry Thomas. Dale, first of all, I want to thank you for believing in this project and the excitement you have shown. I am also thankful for the careful work of editing, layout, and design that has gone into this project.

Contents

Introduction

Interest in health is exploding. Tens of thousands of people are becoming interested in improving their health and reducing the risk of chronic diseases such as heart disease, cancer, stroke, and diabetes. Scientific research continues to point to a highly refined diet as a major culprit in today's killer diseases. Our Natural Lifestyle Cooking plant-based nutrition classes are designed with your health in mind. It is our desire for you to live a longer, happier, and healthier life.

When I conducted my first cooking school in 1969, I had no idea that the experience would be the beginning of a lifelong career of conducting nutrition classes. I have conducted more than 250 nutrition classes with more than twenty thousand attendees and tens of thousands more watching live via satellite and on television. My husband often joins me in these classes, sharing valuable scientific research studies and health tips. It continues to be a real joy for us to help others in their journey to a more healthful lifestyle. We have intentionally prepared this *Natural Lifestyle Cooking Workbook* and the companion *Natural Lifestyle Cooking* cookbook so that many others can enjoy the benefits of good health and teach these health principles as well. I invite you to join us as we demonstrate these recipes, taste this delicious food, and share principles of good nutrition and health.

Too often people focus on their health only when they have health problems. Why not take preventive measures and get on the road to better health before you get sick? You will be glad you did. The following story illustrates the real need to prevent disease rather than deal with it after you have become ill.

Situated on top of a cliff overlooking the emerald-blue waters of the Mediterranean is an ancient Portuguese monastery. The view is breathtaking. The scenery is magnificent. But there is one problem. The only way to get to the top of the cliff is in an old wicker basket tied to a rope and hoisted up by an aged monk. One day a guide and visitor were leaving the monastery. As they stepped into the basket and were lowered down by the monk, the rope swung out over the jagged rocks below. Nervously the tourist asked, "How often do they replace the rope?" "Don't worry," the guide replied in a reassuring tone, "every time one breaks, we replace it."

What a parable of our time. Thousands of people place themselves in a precarious situation regarding their health. They wait until their health snaps, then frantically hope to restore it. The problem is that broken health is not as easily replaced as a snapped rope! Health is not a matter of chance. It is largely a matter of making the right choices and obeying nature's laws.

NUTRITION AND YOUR HEALTH

Although infectious diseases were the major killers in the Western world one hundred years ago, a radical change has occurred in the twenty-first century. The leading killers now are the degenerative diseases such as heart disease, cancer, and stroke. This may not seem like good news; however, it is now possible to reverse this trend by making right lifestyle choices. According to Dr. Caldwell Esselstyn Jr., director of the Cardiovascular Disease Reversal and Prevention Program at Cleveland Clinic Wellness Institute says, "Eighty-five percent of common, chronic, killing diseases in Western civilization are diet-related."[1] Fat and sugar consumption have risen to the point where they comprise at least 40 percent of the American diet.

In these classes we will share a natural diet of fruits, nuts and seeds, grains, and vegetables. These plant-based foods not only contain adequate protein, lots of fiber, plenty of vitamins and minerals, but they also have disease-fighting antioxidants.

Let me commend you on the wise choice you have made to attend these Natural Lifestyle Cooking classes. During our classes we will present scientifically proven, common sense, and widely accepted principles of nutrition. You will discover how to prepare healthy, delicious, and well-balanced plant-based meals that will bring mealtime enjoyment and may add years to your life.

IN THIS SERIES OF NUTRITION CLASSES WE WILL ASSIST YOU IN:

1. INCREASING your consumption of plant-based foods,
2. REDUCING your overall fat consumption,
3. REDUCING your sugar consumption,
4. REPLACING meats with vegetarian proteins,
5. PREPARING delicious, well-balanced, and natural-food dishes,
6. INCREASING the overall amount of fiber and whole grains in your diet,
7. MAKING breakfast a better meal,
8. REDUCING your food costs,
9. CONTROLLING your weight.

There may be some who are studying this workbook and not attending one of our cooking classes. You also desire to make changes in your lifestyle. We commend you for the great choice you have made. We believe your health will improve as you put in practice the principles and information we are sharing. You will also be benefited as you try these simple, delicious plant-based recipes in the companion volume, the *Natural Lifestyle Cooking* cookbook. You will discover the great variety there is in a total vegetarian diet. You will also discover how great the food tastes and enjoy the benefits of feeling better. A healthful diet often gives us more energy and adds years to our lives. It is our wish that you will really enjoy each Natural Lifestyle Cooking class and incorporate these principles into your life so that as the Bible writer says, "You may prosper in all things and be in health" (3 John 2).

ENDNOTE

1. *Vibrant Life,* May/June 2011.

Homemade Breadmaking Made Easy

Breads • Grains • Fiber

Our first session is titled "Homemade Breadmaking Made Easy." Bread is the staff of life. "More and more Americans are saying yes to whole grains. Since 2010, roughly 55 percent of consumers have ditched white bread for whole-wheat or whole-grain varieties, according to the Shopping for Health 2012 Survey, released in July by the Food Marketing Institute and *Prevention* magazine."[1] You can join the large number of health-conscious Americans who not only purchase but also make their own whole-grain bread. This lesson will provide the information that you need to make your own nutritious homemade bread simply and efficiently.

Why take the time and energy to make your own bread when you can easily purchase it? What are the advantages of good homemade whole-grain bread? Is white bread as nutritiously healthy as whole-grain bread? What about the enriching process—does it make white bread superior to whole-grain bread? These are all good questions. Let's explore some answers.

ADVANTAGES OF HOMEMADE WHOLE-GRAIN BREAD
Whole-grain breads are excellent sources of dietary fiber.

1. WHAT IS FIBER?

Fiber is the coarse, structural portion of plant foods that our bodies can't digest or absorb. It is sometimes called roughage. Although fiber is not digestible, it plays a positive role in our overall health. It assists the body in a variety of ways, including disposing of excess fat and toxins. When we increase our fiber intake, we decrease the risk of health conditions such as *cardiovascular disease, stroke, cancer, diabetes, and even obesity.*

2. HOW MUCH FIBER SHOULD WE GET EACH DAY?

Dietary fiber is a vital part of good nutrition. Reading nutrition labels helps us learn how much fiber is in our favorite foods. Concentrate on increasing your fiber intake by eating

more fiber-rich foods. Studies support the American Dietetic Association's position that adults should consume between *25 to 38 grams of fiber a day* from a variety of plant-based foods.[2]

Unfortunately, the average American is not eating adequate amounts of high-fiber foods such as fruits, vegetables, whole grains, and legumes. "Though dietary fiber provides many health benefits, the Harvard School of Public Health states that the average American consumes only about 15 [grams] of fiber each day. This is most likely due to the fact that the typical American diet includes too many fast foods and processed foods like chips, crackers, candy and pastries."[3]

"A diet adequate in fiber-containing foods is also usually rich in micronutrients and nonnutritive ingredients that have additional health benefits. It is unclear why several recently published clinical trials with dietary fiber intervention failed to show a reduction in colon polyps. Nonetheless, a fiber-rich diet is associated with a lower risk of colon cancer. A fiber-rich meal is processed more slowly, which promotes earlier satiety, and is frequently less calorically dense and lower in fat and added sugars. All of these characteristics are features of a dietary pattern to treat and prevent obesity."[4]

3. WHAT FOODS ARE HIGH IN FIBER?

A. _____

B. _____

C. _____

If you would like to include more fiber in your diet, a plant-based diet is extremely beneficial. Consciously choose more *fruits, vegetables, legumes, and whole grains.* Even try making your own whole-grain bread. You will be glad you did.

HIGH-FIBER FOODS

4. WHAT MAJOR DISEASES DOES FIBER ASSIST IN PREVENTING?

A. _____

B. _____

C. _____

In a well-researched article published on the Harvard University School of Public Health's Web site, The Nutrition Source, October 3, 2012, titled "Fiber: Start Roughing It!" the value of fiber is clearly stated: "High intake of dietary fiber has been linked to a lower risk of heart disease in a number of large studies that followed people for many years. In a Harvard study of over 40,000 male health professionals, researchers found that a high total dietary fiber intake was linked to a 40 percent lower risk of coronary heart disease, compared to a low fiber intake. Cereal fiber, which is found in grains, seemed particularly beneficial. A related Harvard study of female nurses produced quite similar findings."[5]

"One question raised by such studies is whether fiber itself protects against heart disease and diabetes, or whether the disease-fighting benefits accrue from the nutrient-rich whole grain package. A recent meta-analysis of seven major studies showed that cardiovascular disease (heart attack, stroke, or the need for a procedure to bypass or open a clogged artery) was 21 percent less likely in people who ate 2.5 or more servings of whole grain foods a day compared with those who ate less than 2 servings a week. Another meta-analysis of several large studies, including more than 700,000 men and women, found that eating an extra 2 servings of whole grains a day decreased the risk of type 2 diabetes by 21 percent. So to protect against heart disease and diabetes, perhaps the best advice is to choose whole-grain, high-fiber foods at most meals."[6]

Eating whole grains instead of highly refined, processed foods lowers the total cholesterol, triglyceride, and insulin levels. These reductions combine to reduce the risk of coronary artery disease.[7] "In the Harvard-based Nurses' Health Study, women who ate 2 to 3 servings of whole-grain products (mostly bread and breakfast cereals) each day were 30 percent less likely to have a heart attack or die from heart disease over a 10-year period than women who ate less than 1 serving per week."[8]

Consider the vitamin and mineral loss in processed flour reported on pages 20 and 21 of the *Natural Lifestyle Cooking* cookbook. More than *half of the B vitamins, 50 percent of the calcium, and virtually all of the fiber are removed in the enriching process,* along with multiple other key nutrients.

"In a 10-year Harvard [University] study completed in 1994, men and women who ate high-fiber breads had fewer strokes and heart attacks. . . . Simply switching from white to whole wheat bread can lower heart disease risk by 20 percent, according to research from the University of Washington reported in the April 2, 2003 issue of the *Journal of the American Medical Association.*"[9]

There are many health benefits in making your own bread. It is not only delicious but nutritious. And fresh baked bread smells so good. Try it. Breadmaking is really not that difficult. You will find several recipes in the *Natural Lifestyle Cooking* cookbook on pages 19–38.

HOMEMADE WHOLE-GRAIN BREAD

Foods that contain dietary fiber include fruits, vegetables, nuts, grains, and legumes. One of the best ways to boost fiber intake is to eat several servings of whole grains, fruits, vegetables, and legumes, such as beans and lentils, every day. This may require a change in your eating habits, but it will reward you with health dividends. Include a variety of high-fiber foods in your diet daily.

EAT AN ABUNDANCE OF THESE HIGH-FIBER FOODS

"Looking to add more fiber to your diet? Fiber—along with adequate fluid intake—moves quickly and relatively easily through your digestive tract and helps it function properly. A high-fiber diet may also help reduce the risk of obesity, heart disease and diabetes."[10] The following chart, prepared by the Mayo Clinic staff, comparing the amount of fiber in various plant-based foods is helpful.[11] It can assist in making wiser food choices. In addition to whole-grain bread, choose the high-fiber plant-based foods found in the chart, and you will get plenty of fiber.

(See pages 40, 41 in *Natural Lifestyle Cooking* cookbook for additional information on fiber.)

MAYO CLINIC FIBER CHART

	Serving size	Total fiber (grams)*
FRUITS		
Raspberries	1 cup	8.0
Pear, with skin	1 medium	5.5
Apple, with skin	1 medium	4.4
Banana	1 medium	3.1
Orange	1 medium	3.1
Strawberries (halves)	1 cup	3.0
Figs, dried	2 medium	1.6
Raisins	1 oz. (60 raisins)	1.0
GRAINS, CEREAL, AND PASTA		
Spaghetti, whole-wheat, cooked	1 cup	6.3
Barley, pearled, cooked	1 cup	6.0
Bran flakes	$3/4$ cup	5.3
Oat bran muffin	1 medium	5.2
Oatmeal, instant, cooked	1 cup	4.0
Popcorn, air-popped	3 cups	3.5
Brown rice, cooked	1 cup	3.5
Bread, rye	1 slice	1.9
Bread, whole-wheat or multigrain	1 slice	1.9
LEGUMES, NUTS, AND SEEDS		
Split peas, cooked	1 cup	16.3
Lentils, cooked	1 cup	15.6
Black beans, cooked	1 cup	15.0
Lima beans, cooked	1 cup	13.2
Baked beans, vegetarian, canned, cooked	1 cup	10.4
Sunflower seed kernels	$1/4$ cup	3.9
Almonds	1 oz. (23 nuts)	3.5
Pistachio nuts	1 oz. (49 nuts)	2.9
Pecans	1 oz. (19 halves)	2.7
VEGETABLES		
Artichoke, cooked	1 medium	10.3
Green peas, cooked	1 cup	8.8
Broccoli, boiled	1 cup	5.1
Turnip greens, boiled	1 cup	5.0
Brussels sprouts, cooked	1 cup	4.1
Sweet corn, cooked	1 cup	4.0
Potato, with skin, baked	1 small	3.0
Tomato paste	$1/4$ cup	2.7
Carrot, raw	1 medium	1.7

* Fiber content can vary between brands.

Whole—grain breads are an excellent source of B vitamins.

5. WHAT IS ONE OF THE GREATEST BENEFITS OF THE B-COMPLEX VITAMINS?

A *deficiency in the B-complex vitamins* has been shown *to produce heightened anxiety, increased tension, and greater irritability.* Studies done on people with inadequate B vitamins reveal they are also more prone to discouragement and depression. A lack of B vitamins also contributes to an inability to concentrate and focus one's thoughts.

WHOLE-GRAIN BREAD IS FULL OF B VITAMINS
Homemade whole-grain breads contain the natural goodness packaged by our loving Creator. Nutrients are not depleted by processing and then artificially replaced.

6. WHAT ARE SOME OF THE VITAMINS AND MINERALS THAT ARE LOST IN THE REFINING PROCESS?

_____

_____

_____

VITAMIN AND MINERAL LOSS IN PROCESSED FLOUR[12]

VITAMIN OR MINERAL	Percent Lost
Vitamin B_1 (Thiamine)	86 percent
Vitamin B_2 (Riboflavin)	70 percent
Niacin	86 percent
Iron	84 percent
Vitamin B_6 (Pyridoxine)	60 percent
Folic Acid	70 percent
Pantothenic Acid	54 percent
Biotin	90 percent
Calcium	50 percent
Phosphorous	78 percent
Copper	75 percent
Magnesium	72 percent
Manganese	71 percent

A large number of nutrients are lost in the refining process, and the United States Food and Drug Administration requires only five to be added back. So much fiber is lost in the refining process that you would have to eat eight pieces of white bread to get the fiber found in just one piece of whole-wheat bread.

7. WHAT SPECIFIC ESSENTIAL NUTRIENTS ARE ADDED IN THE ENRICHING PROCESS TO COMPENSATE FOR THE LOSS OF NATURAL NUTRIENTS DURING THE REFINING PROCESS?

A. _____

B. _____

C. _____

D. _____

E. _____

F. _____ (OCCASIONALLY)

The widespread use of refined white flour began in the late 1800s. Food analysts discovered that removing the germ from wheat kept the flour from going rancid. In the 1940s, the United States recognized that white flour was nutritionally deficient. People who ate it began developing health problems such as beriberi, a disease caused by vitamin B_1 or thiamine deficiency. The United States government then regulated the refining of wheat. It required manufacturers to enrich their white flour by adding *thiamine, iron, niacin, and riboflavin. Folic acid* was added to the list later. In some cases, *calcium may be added,* but about thirty nutrients were removed from the wheat with only a few added back in the enriching process.

Enrichment might be compared to a thief stealing twenty-five dollars from you, then feeling guilty and giving you five dollars back. Would you feel enriched? Certainly not! You would probably be thankful to get some of the money back, but you would certainly wish the entire amount had been returned. By using whole grains, you can get all of the vitamins and minerals that our loving Creator included in the first place.

WHOLE-WHEAT BREAD

8. WHAT ARE THE RESULTS OF THIAMINE DEFICIENCY?

A. _____

B. _____

C. _____

Vitamin B₁ or thiamine deficiency causes beriberi, a nervous symptom ailment. Symptoms of this disease include *weight loss and emotional disturbances.* Lack of thiamine causes an *impairment of the short-term memory.* Thiamine deficiency also causes weakness and pain in the limbs, periods of irregular heartbeat, and edema, which is the swelling of body tissues. Heart failure and death may occur in advanced cases.[13] Chronic thiamine deficiency can also cause some neurological disorders. B vitamins are vital to our health and optimum well-being.

DIET AND DISPOSITION

Recent studies have confirmed that a good diet with adequate whole grains significantly influences behavior. The link between diet and disposition has been well known for decades. As early as the 1940s, Dr. Roger Williams, formerly of the University of Texas at Austin, discovered a definite relationship between negative behavior and a lack of thiamine in the diet.[14]

Get some of your grams of fiber with these delicious **PECAN ROLLS.** See the recipe in the Holidays and Special Occasions section on page 112.

Combine the **PECAN ROLLS** with one cup of **PEA SOUP** (*Natural Lifestyle Cooking* cookbook, page 124) and you have a meal packed with fiber.

Homemade whole—grain breads are free from some of the artificial preservatives, additives, and dairy products that are often present in commercially prepared breads.

Most commercial breads contain potentially harmful preservatives, additives, and dairy products.

ARTIFICIAL SWEETENERS: Artificial sweeteners often claim to replace sugar without containing extra calories. Many of these artificial sweeteners contain a large mixture of unhealthful chemicals.

MILK CONTAMINANTS: Milk often contains contaminants ranging from pesticides to drugs. Synthetic hormones such as recombinant bovine growth hormone (rBGH) are commonly used in dairy cows to increase the production of milk. Pesticides, polychlorinated biphenyls (PCBs), and dioxins are other examples of contaminants found in milk. These toxins affect the immune and reproductive systems. The central nervous system can also be affected. PCBs and dioxins have also been linked to cancer.[15]

Hundreds of man-made chemicals are added to our American food supply today. Food additives are not natural nutrition for humans. Make it a habit to *read labels.* You may be surprised at what is actually in the food you are eating each day.

No wonder many of the store-bought breads don't mold anymore. You can keep them for several weeks, and they won't go bad because there are so many preservatives in them. Recently, I tested this myself. I bought what appeared to be good commercial bread. I left it in the pantry for literally weeks—and it didn't go bad. In fact, there was no sign of spoilage. I was shocked at how many preservatives had to be in the bread in order to keep it so long. To understand what you purchase, *read labels.* Beware when there are a host of ingredients you can't pronounce and don't understand.

MAKING HOMEMADE BREAD

If you want to eat more healthfully, try making your own homemade bread. Breadmaking can be easy and fun. Remember, though, it will keep fresh for only about a week. Let's take a look at the basic ingredients used in various kinds of breads. Once you have these basic ingredients, you can exchange the kind of whole-grain flour to vary your bread. You can also add other ingredients such as nuts and oats for extra protein.

BASIC INGREDIENTS USED IN ALMOST ALL BREADS

YEAST: Yeast is essential in breadmaking. It helps the bread rise. When warm water is added to the yeast, it begins to grow. As it grows, it combines with the sweetening that is in the flour and produces carbon dioxide. This gas expands the dough and makes little bubbles that are trapped in the dough. When wheat flour containing gluten is added, it makes the dough elastic so it can stretch instead of break when the bubbles are formed. The bubbles make the dough rise. Therefore, yeast is an essential ingredient in making leavened bread. Activate the active dry yeast in warm water at about 110°F.

LIQUID: Water is the best liquid to use in bread and is the most economical. Water helps to combine the ingredients. It also aids in activating yeast that releases carbon dioxide.

SWEETENERS: Sweetening is primarily used to add flavor to the bread. It also contributes to the browning of bread. Sweetening also promotes tenderness and gives the yeast something to feed on. The sweeteners we have used in *Natural Lifestyle Cooking* include brown sugar, honey, maple syrup, molasses, and fruits such as applesauce.

SALT: Salt adds flavor and helps to control the rising of the bread by strengthening the gluten in the flour.

OIL: Oil makes the bread more moist and tender. It also helps extend the shelf life. However, it is possible to make oil-free bread by substituting an apple or applesauce. You may want to try this once you have mastered the art of breadmaking.

FLOUR: Flour is the most important ingredient in breadmaking. Flour contains gluten, which is a protein that provides for the elasticity and the basic structure of bread. The grain most commonly used is wheat flour. Remember, wheat flour refers to white as well as whole wheat. Read labels. Be sure the label says "whole wheat" or you may get fewer nutrients than you thought. Using *100 percent whole-grain flour provides the best nutritional value* for your bread. Other

nonwheat flours, such as quinoa, millet, rye, and oats can also be used. Because some flours do not contain gluten, it is important that they are mixed with large amounts of wheat flour.

BASIC INGREDIENTS IN BREAD
Homemade whole-grain breads are less expensive than commercially baked bread. You will save on your food budget.

9. WHAT IS THE APPROXIMATE DIFFERENCE IN PRICE BETWEEN STORE-BOUGHT WHOLE-GRAIN BREAD AND HOMEMADE WHOLE-GRAIN BREAD?

_____

APPROXIMATE PRICE COMPARISON OF HOMEMADE BREAD AND STORE-BOUGHT BREAD

COST OF HOMEMADE WHOLE-GRAIN BREAD		COST OF STORE BOUGHT WHOLE-GRAIN BREAD	
2 Loaves		1 Loaf	
Water	$0.00	Arnold's 100 % whole wheat	$2.50
Active dry yeast	$0.16	Nature's Own 100% whole wheat	$2.99
Honey	$0.40	Double Fiber 100% whole wheat	$3.19
Salt	$0.02		
Light olive oil	$0.12		
Whole-wheat flour	$1.20		
Total for 2 loaves	$1.90		
Average cost per loaf = $0.95 homemade bread		Average cost per loaf = $2.89 store-bought whole-wheat bread	

(Note: If you use brown sugar, it is even less expensive.)

RAISIN BREAD, DINNER ROLLS, and **PECAN ROLLS**
Homemade whole-grain bread has a wonderful flavor and great texture.

Whole-Grain **OATMEAL-PECAN BREAD**
Whole-grain breadmaking provides warm memories.

Tips for Making Good-Textured Homemade Bread

1. When making 100 percent whole-wheat bread, you can *add approximately ½ cup of vital wheat gluten* to 7 or more cups of whole-wheat flour.

2. If you are making bread *for the first time, add a little unbleached enriched flour* to your whole-grain bread. The gluten in it will make a softer, better texture. Replace some of the nutrients lost by adding wheat germ.

3. One of the keys to making good homemade bread is to be sure to *add the last 2 cups of flour gradually.* Excess flour makes bread heavier. Use only enough of the flour called for in a recipe to prevent the dough from sticking to your hands. You may or may not need all the flour called for in a recipe. The amount of flour needed can change due to weather or altitude.

4. *Add 1 to 2 cups potato water* or mashed potatoes to your bread to give it a good texture.

5. *Use an emulsifier.* A common emulsifier used in baking is lecithin. Using an emulsifier like lecithin will prevent the starch in the flour from recrystallizing, which makes the bread dry and stale.

6. *Practice.* Practice makes perfect. Find a recipe you like and make it over and over again. If you keep making it, you will get better and better at it. And best of all—your family will love it too.

The texture and flavor of a good loaf of homemade whole-grain bread is hard to beat.

Good-Textured Homemade **RYE BREAD**
Freshly baked homemade whole-grain bread not only
has an aroma that is delightful, it is nutritiously satisfying.

10. WHY DOES EATING WHOLE-GRAIN BREAD HELP A PERSON FEEL SATISFIED?

Whole-grain bread provides many important nutrients. Whole grains are filled with vitamins, minerals, protein, carbohydrates, and fiber that meet our nutritional needs and satisfy our hunger.

There is nothing quite like the smell and taste of homemade bread to give your house a warm and welcoming feeling. Serving homemade bread creates a positive atmosphere. Most family members really appreciate it when you make homemade bread. Your family will love it and so will the friends you invite home to enjoy a good slice of homemade whole-wheat bread. Making homemade bread provides a great sense of accomplishment for the family members who participate in making it with you. Bread bakers are always on everyone's favorite list. The gift of a loaf of freshly baked homemade bread and delicious wheat rolls are highly appreciated by most people.

Family fellowship seems to be a lost art in today's fast-paced society. The smell of freshly baked bread invites families to relax and share a meal together. Family relationships are very important factors for our health. Getting adequate nutrients, especially B vitamins, affects our dispositions and the way we relate to our families and others.

RECIPE USING VARIOUS WHOLE GRAINS

Health Bread

2 T. (2 pkg.) active dry yeast
½ c. warm water
2 ¾ c. boiling water
¾ c. molasses or honey
1 T. salt
2 T. olive oil
¼ c. ground flaxseed

1 c. wheat germ
1 c. quick oats
1 c. bran
1 c. barley flour
½ c. millet flour
3 c. whole-wheat flour
1 to 2 c. unbleached enriched flour

MIX active yeast in ½ cup warm water. In a second bowl, COMBINE boiling water, molasses, salt, olive oil, flaxseed, wheat germ, oats, bran, barley flour, and millet flour. STIR in yeast. BEAT well. ADD whole-wheat flour to make moderately stiff dough. ADD unbleached enriched flour gradually. TURN OUT on a lightly floured surface. KNEAD until smooth and satiny. SHAPE dough into a ball. PLACE in lightly greased bowl. COVER and let rise in warm place until double (about 1 ½ hours). PUNCH down. CUT into 2 portions. (For smaller loaves, cut it into 3 portions.) SHAPE into loaves. LET RISE until double (about 1 hour). BAKE 30 to 35 minutes at 350°F.

Know Your Grains

It is important to know the various grains that are available. *Whole grains are economical, nutritious, and delicious.* They have sustained and nourished the world for many years. *Whole grains are high-energy foods.* Scientific evidence demonstrates that consuming whole grains can help prevent many twenty-first-century killer diseases. A diet with plentiful amounts of varied grains puts us on the road to good health. Let's look at some of the most familiar whole grains, their nutrient contents, and their uses and benefits.

BARLEY: Whole-grain barley is a healthy high-protein, high-fiber whole grain. It has a chewy texture.

- **NUTRIENT CONTENTS:** 1 cup of cooked barley contains 6 grams of fiber and 4 grams of protein with approximately 193 calories.[16]
- **BENEFITS:** Improves digestion and reduces cholesterol.

BUCKWHEAT: Buckwheat kernels are hulled seeds of the buckwheat plant. Although buckwheat is technically a fruit, it is used as a grain. Buckwheat flour is more commonly used for pancakes. However, because it is a heavier flour, it is best when mixed with other grains.

- **NUTRIENT CONTENTS:** Buckwheat has several nutrients, including the minerals phosphorus, iron, and potassium. It also contains vitamin E and B vitamins.
- **BENEFITS:** Because buckwheat is not part of the wheat family, it can be used by people on a wheat-free diet.

CORN: Corn is a grain known in many countries as maize.

- **NUTRIENT CONTENTS:** 1 cup of corn contains 4.6 grams of fiber. In research studies, corn intake is often associated with good overall fiber intake.
- **BENEFITS:** Protects the mucosa of the digestive tract and reduces cholesterol levels. Fiber in corn is one of the keys to well-documented digestive benefits. Corn is important in overall antioxidant protection and is also a contributing factor in reducing the risk of cardiovascular disease.

  According to the Web site the World's Healthiest Foods, "Recent research has shown that corn can support the growth of friendly bacteria in our large intestine and can also be transformed by these bacteria into short chain fatty acids, or SCFAs. These SCFAs can supply energy to our intestinal cells and thereby help lower our risk of intestinal problems, including our risk of colon cancer."[17]

MILLET: Millet has been a staple food for thousands of years and was used during ancient times to make bread. It is mentioned in the Bible. Today millet ranks as one of the important grains in the world, although it is not used as widely in the United States. In the United States, it is more widely known and used as birdseed or cattle feed. *Millet is a highly nutritious, healthful, and versatile grain* that would be a great addition to our diet.

Note: The Hunzakuts, who live in the Himalayan foothills, are known for their excellent health and longevity. This long-living population group enjoys millet as a staple in their diet.

- **NUTRIENT CONTENTS:** Millet is filled with nutrients. It contains magnesium, calcium, phosphorus, fiber, B vitamins, and antioxidants.

- **BENEFITS:** Millet is a highly nutritious, nonacid-forming food. "Millet is a good source of several alkalinizing minerals. In the USDA Nutrient Database, 3.5 ounces of millet is listed as providing 119 mg of magnesium and 14 mg of calcium. These two minerals support the acid/alkaline balance within the body and are needed when the blood becomes too acidic."[18]

  It is easy to digest. In fact, millet is considered one of the least allergenic and most digestible grains available. Millet contains about 11 percent protein, which is higher than wheat, rice, and corn. Millet is often used by people on wheat-free diets.

  (Note: We will emphasize recipes using millet.)

OATS: Oats are a hardy cereal grain known scientifically as *Avena sativa*.

- **NUTRIENT CONTENTS:** One cup of oats contains 17 grams of fiber. Oats are filled with vitamins such as thiamine, riboflavin, niacin, B_6, and with minerals such as calcium, magnesium, iron, phosphorus, potassium, zinc, and copper. Oats are also rich in protein.

- **BENEFITS:** A study published in the *Archives of Internal Medicine* confirms that eating high-fiber foods, such as oats, whole grains, fruits, and vegetables helps reduce overall mortality. The study states, "We found that dietary fiber from grains was significantly inversely related to the risk of total, CVD [cardiovascular disease], cancer, and respiratory disease death in both men and women. Comparing the highest to the lowest intake of fiber from grains, men had a 22% lower risk of total death . . . and women had a 19% lower risk of total death."[19]

Whole grains make a significant difference in reducing disease and our longevity.

QUINOA: Quinoa is pronounced *KEEN-wah* and has the *highest protein content of all the whole grains,* so it is an excellent food for those on a plant-based diet. Quinoa provides all nine essential amino acids, making it a complete protein. Quinoa is a cholesterol-free, gluten free whole grain. Although it is usually considered to be a whole grain, it is actually a seed but is used like a whole grain.

- **NUTRIENT CONTENTS:** Quinoa contains more protein than wheat or corn. It is a good source of dietary fiber, a good source of phosphorus, and is high in magnesium and iron. It also contains iron, potassium, magnesium, zinc, and other minerals.[20]

- **BENEFITS:** The nutrients in quinoa are important for heart, nerve, and muscle function. Quinoa can be used in breadmaking and also in various kinds of entrées.

(Note: Quinoa is used in the **QUINOA PATTIES** on page 79.)

RICE: Brown rice is a kind of whole grain. When only the outermost layer of a grain of rice (the husk) is removed, the product is brown rice. To produce white rice, the next layers underneath the husk, the bran and germ layers are removed, leaving mostly the starchy endosperm. Several vitamins and dietary minerals are lost in this removal and polishing process. Therefore, to get the most nutrition, it is important to eat brown rice rather than white rice. It is gluten free and can be easily eaten by most people.

- **NUTRIENT CONTENTS:** Brown rice provides a healthy amount of fiber, calcium, iron, magnesium, phosphorus, potassium, manganese, and selenium.
- **BENEFITS:** The fiber and selenium found in brown rice can also reduce your risk of many types of cancer. Oils found in brown rice can help lower cholesterol.

RYE: Rye is a grain used to produce flour. Rye bread, including pumpernickel, is used widely in northern and eastern Europe. It has lower gluten content than wheat flour. However, it can be nicely combined with whole-wheat flour to make delicious, nutritious rye bread. You will find a recipe for rye bread on page 30 in the *Natural Lifestyle Cooking* cookbook.

- **NUTRIENT CONTENTS:** Rye is a good source of vitamin E, calcium, iron, thiamine, phosphorus, and potassium. It is particularly a good source of dietary fiber.
- **BENEFITS:** The nutrients in rye are needed for overall health. Dr. Celeste Robb-Nicholson, editor in chief of *Harvard Women's Health Watch,* says, "Try to get most of your vitamin E from food. There's strong evidence that diets containing large amounts of vitamin E-rich foods are good for you."[21]

SPELT: Spelt is a grain with a light, nutty, and delicious flavor. Spelt contains protein and has a considerable amount of B vitamins, magnesium, and fiber.

WHEAT: Wheat is a grain that is grown on more land area than any other commercial crop and is *one of the most important staple foods* for humans.[22] World trade in wheat is greater than for all other crops combined. Wheat is probably the king of all the grains. All of the recipes on pages 24–35 in the *Natural Lifestyle Cooking* cookbook contain some whole wheat. Try making some good whole-grain bread. It will add a great source of fiber to your diet.

- **NUTRIENT CONTENTS:** Whole wheat contains protein, fiber, vitamins, and minerals. The germ and bran contain vitamins such as B_1, B_2, B_6, niacin, and E. Also calcium, magnesium, iron, and zinc are contained in wheat.
- **BENEFITS:** Whole wheat helps protect against diseases such as arteriosclerosis, cancer, and diabetes.

> *Because whole grains should be an integral part of our diet, it is important to be aware of the many different grains that can be used both for breakfast and breadmaking. It would be well to use a mixture of the various whole grains.*

As you continue on your journey to good health and put these principles of healthful living into practice, you will quickly begin to notice the benefits. *Your health will improve.* Your energy level will increase. Your thinking will become clearer. You will feel more alert and positive about life.

Eating a nutritious, tasty, natural diet will produce both a healthy mind and a healthy body. Truly the ancient Scriptures are right when they declare, "Blessed are you, O land, when your king is the son of nobles, and your princes feast at the proper time—for strength and not for drunkenness" (Ecclesiastes 10:17). Eating for strength and not for mere gratification of appetite produces physical health and mental joy.

In our upcoming sessions, we will study additional basic principles of healthy eating that will not only transform your dietary practices to reduce the risk of disease but they will also revolutionize your way of thinking, enabling you to become a more contented, self-controlled, and cheerful person. Jesus said, "I am the bread of life" (John 6:48).

He also declared, "It is written, 'Man shall not live by bread alone, but by every word that proceeds from the mouth of God' " (Matthew 4:4). Good whole-grain homemade bread satisfies the nutritional needs of the body, just as Jesus satisfies our inner spiritual needs.

ANSWERS TO CLASS 1

1. Fiber is indigestible vegetable cellular material contained in food.
2. Twenty-five to thirty-eight grams daily
3. A. Fruits and vegetables
    B. Legumes (beans, peas, lentils, etc.)
    C. Whole grains
4. A. Heart disease
    B. Stroke
    C. Type 2 diabetes
5. They help stabilize the nervous system.
6. See the chart on page 15.
7. A. Thiamine
    B. Riboflavin
    C. Niacin
    D. Folic acid
    E. Iron
    F. Calcium may be added to some enriched flours.

8. A. Weight loss
    B. Emotional disturbances
    C. Impaired short-term memory

9. Triple

10. The bread provided adequate nutrients and fiber.

ENDNOTES

1.   Bonnie Taub-Dix, "Whole Grains, Whole Diet," Eat + Run, *U.S. News and World Report,* September 6, 2012, http://health.USNews.com/health-news/blogs/eat-run/2012/09/06whole-grains-whole-diet.

2.   Sarah Davis, "Daily Recommended Fiber Intake," Live Strong, accessed March 25, 2013, http://www.livestrong.com/article/82725-daily-recommended-fiber-intake.

3.   Ibid.

4.   Judith A. Marlett, Michael I. McBurney, and Joanne L. Slavin, "Position of the American Dietetic Association: Health Implications of Dietary Fiber," *Journal of the American Dietetic Association* 102, no. 7 (July 2002): 993–1000.

5.   Harvard University School of Public Health, "Fiber: Start Roughing It!" The Nutrition Source, accessed March 23, 2013, http://www.hsph.harvard.edu/nutritionsource/fiber-full-story/.

6.   Ibid.

7.   "Whole Grains: The Inside Story," *Nutrition Action Healthletter,* May 2006, accessed March 26, 2013, http://www.cspinet.org/nah/05_06/grains.pdf; David R. Jacobs Jr. et al., "Whole-Grain Intake May Reduce the Risk of Ischemic Heart Disease Death in Postmenopausal Women: The Iowa Women's Health Study," *American Journal of Nutrition* 68, no. 2 (1998): 248–257.

8.   Simin Liu et al., "Whole-Grain Consumption and Risk of Coronary Heart Disease: Results From the Nurses' Health Study," *American Journal of Clinical Nutrition* 70, no. 3 (1999): 412–419, cited in Harvard University School of Public Health, "Health Gains From Whole Grains," The Nutrition Source, accessed July 1, 2013, http://www.hsph.harvard.edu/nutritionsource/health-gains-from-whole-grains/.

9.   Dariush Mozaffarian et al., "Cereal, Fruit, and Vegetable Fiber Intake and the Risk of Cardiovascular Disease in Elderly Individuals," *Journal of the American Medical Association* 289, no. 13 (April 2, 2003): 1659–1666, cited in Lisa Barley, "White Bread Vs. Wheat Bread," *Vegetarian Times,* accessed March 27, 2013, http://www.vegetariantimes.com/article/white-bread-vs-wheat-bread/.

10. Mayo Clinic staff, "Chart of High-Fiber Foods," Mayo Clinic, accessed March 27, 2013, http://www.mayoclinic.com/health/high-fiber-foods/NU00582.

11. Ibid.

12. Compiled from M. G. Hardinge and H. Crooks, "Lesser Known Vitamins in Foods," *Journal of the American Dietetic Association* 38 (April 1961): 240–243..

13. Wikipedia contributors, "Beriberi," *Wikipedia,* accessed July 2, 2013, http://en.wikipedia.org/wiki/Beriberi.

14. Roger Williams, "The Approximate Vitamin Requirements of Human Beings," *Journal of the American Medical Association* 119, no. 1 (May 1942): 1–3.

15. A. J. Baars et al., "Dioxins, Dioxin-like PCBs and Non-dioxin-like PCBs in Foodstuffs: Occurrence and Dietary Intake in the Netherlands," *Toxicology Letters* 151, no. 1 (June 15, 2004): 51–61.

16. "Barley, Pearled, Cooked," Self Nutrition Data, accessed March 27, 2013, http://nutritiondata.self.com/facts/cereal-grains-and-pasta/5680/2.

17. "Corn," The World's Healthiest Foods, accessed March 28, 2013, http://www.whfoods.com/genpage.php?tname=foodspice&dbid=90.

18. Joel Le Blanc, "Does Eating Millet Help Rid Body of Acid Ash?" Live Strong, accessed March 28, 2013, http://www.livestrong.com/article/550217-does-eating-millet-help-rid-body-of-acid-ash/.

19. Y. Park et al., "Dietary Fiber Intake and Mortality in the NIH-AARP Diet and Health Study," *Archives of Internal Medicine* 171, no. 12 (June 27, 2011): 1061–1068.

20. Jolinda Hackett, "Quinoa Nutrition Facts," About.com, accessed March 28, 2013, http://vegetarian.about.com/od/healthnutrition/qt/Quinoa-Nutrition-Facts.htm.

21. "Vitamin E Controversy: Has Vitamin E Fallen from Grace?" *Harvard Health Publications,* accessed July 8, 2013, http://www.health.harvard.edu/press_releases/facts_about_vitamine.

22. Wikipedia contributors, "Wheat," *Wikipedia,* accessed July 8, 2013, http://en.wikipedia.org/wiki/Wheat.

Class 2

Making Breakfast
a Better Meal

Breakfast · Antioxidants

Would you like to increase your life expectancy by as many as eleven years? What price would you pay for an additional eleven happy, healthy years? If it were possible to place the formula for longevity in a pill, would you stand in line with millions of others to purchase your supply? Dr. Lester Breslow, professor emeritus and dean emeritus, Fielding School of Public Health at University of California, Los Angeles, made this startling assertion: it is possible, by following seven basic health guidelines, to increase American life expectancy by eleven years. After conducting extensive research, Dr. Breslow concluded that following the seven principles listed below will add years to your life.

1. Avoid tobacco
2. Limit the use of alcohol, or don't drink at all
3. Eat in moderation
4. Get adequate rest (seven to eight hours per night)
5. Engage in frequent exercise
6. Remain close to your ideal weight
7. Eat a good breakfast every day[1]

Dr. Lester Breslow incorporated these seven principles into his own lifestyle, and they made a difference. He died on April 9, 2012, at the age of ninety-seven. These principles can make a difference in your life too. In this session we will focus on the last of these basic seven health principles—eating a good breakfast.

Many people feel too rushed or too tired to eat a good breakfast. Some are not hungry. Others feel they want to lose weight, and they think that skipping breakfast is a good way to do it.

The American Academy of Family Physicians reviewed the results of a 2004 study conducted by KRC Research on behalf of America's Breakfast Council. The study revealed that although the majority of Americans acknowledge the importance of eating a good breakfast, one-third chose not to eat any breakfast at all.

An additional 25 percent say they eat breakfast only three out of five working days each week. " 'Americans need to make eating a healthy breakfast part of their daily morning ritual,' said Gail Rampersaud, RD. 'By eating a nutrient-rich meal packed with whole grains, protein, fruit or natural fruit juices, like 100 percent orange juice, they can get the nutrition they need to get their day off to a healthy start.' "[2]

"Eating breakfast can help improve children's behavior and school performance, as well as help them maintain a healthy weight. But a survey by the Academy of Nutrition and Dietetics Foundation reveals that breakfast isn't eaten all of the time by 42 percent of Caucasian and Hispanic children, and 59 percent of African American children."[3]

What do these statistics reveal?

- Is there a relationship between a poor-quality breakfast and mental attitudes and academic performance?
- Does the typical American breakfast of bacon and eggs with a cup of coffee, or a breakfast of highly refined, sugar-laden cereal and doughnuts contribute to the Western world's growing epidemic of heart disease, cancer, and diabetes?
- What specific advantages are there in eating a substantial breakfast?
- What composes a nutritionally good breakfast?
- How can we make breakfast a better meal?

In this session we will explore answers to these questions. We will also show you how to prepare a balanced breakfast with numerous tasty options:

- Delicious whole-grain cereals
- A tasty fruit cobbler
- Healthy low-cost granola
- Protein-rich breakfast beans
- Nourishing oatmeal pancakes
- Delightful fresh-fruit dishes
- Nutritious waffles, French toast, and much more

Note: The recipes for these healthy breakfast dishes are found in the *Natural Lifestyle Cooking* cookbook.

VEGETARIANS HAVE PLENTY OF BREAKFAST CHOICES

People eating a plant-based vegetarian diet have many choices for a nutritious breakfast. We have included a few of our favorites in this workbook and many more in the *Natural Lifestyle Cooking* cookbook. A nutritious, substantial breakfast should provide one-third to one-half of the day's total needed calories. Perhaps Mother was right after all when she encouraged us to eat a good breakfast.

REASONS WHY MANY AMERICANS SKIP EATING A GOOD BREAKFAST

1. **WHAT ARE THE BASIC REASONS WHY MANY AMERICANS SKIP BREAKFAST?**

   A. _____

   B. _____

   C. _____

   D. _____

   E. _____

Forty-seven percent of the people who reported skipping breakfast in the America's Breakfast Council survey said they did so because "they do not have enough time or feel that it is too inconvenient."[4]

"People who eat a well-balanced breakfast tend to have more nutritious diets than those who skip breakfast regularly. Breakfast-eaters typically consume foods higher in fiber, vitamins and minerals and avoid foods high in saturated fat and cholesterol," said Liz Weiss, a registered dietitian specializing in health and nutrition.[5]

One of the classic studies on the benefits of a good breakfast is titled "The Iowa Breakfast Studies." This study indicated the detrimental effect of skipping breakfast and the positive benefits of eating a good breakfast. In a pilot program conducted by the U.S. Department of Agriculture on twelve- to fourteen-year-old boys, the results were remarkable. There was a marked difference between those who ate breakfast and those who skipped breakfast.[6]

2. WHAT DID THE IOWA BREAKFAST STUDY SHOW REGARDING THE DETRIMENTAL EFFECTS OF SKIPPING BREAKFAST AND THE POSITIVE BENEFITS OF EATING A GOOD BREAKFAST?

    A. DETRIMENTAL EFFECTS OF SKIPPING BREAKFAST:

        I. _____

        II. _____

    B. BENEFITS OF EATING A GOOD BREAKFAST:

        I. _____

        II. _____

        III. _____

THE ADVANTAGES OF EATING A SUBSTANTIAL BREAKFAST

Breakfast Supplies Energy for the Day's Activities

3. WHY IS IT SO IMPORTANT TO EAT THE RIGHT KIND OF BREAKFAST FOODS?

    A. _____

    B. _____

    C. _____

"The right breakfast foods can help you concentrate, give you strength—even help you maintain a healthy weight. . . . Not only does [breakfast] give you energy to start a new day, but breakfast is linked to many health benefits."[7]

Breakfast provides essential vitamins and minerals, enabling the body to function at peak energy levels throughout the morning.

4. WHY IS IT SO IMPORTANT TO GET ADEQUATE NUTRIENTS EACH MORNING AT BREAKFAST FOR OUR BODIES TO FUNCTION AT OPTIMUM LEVELS?

Getting adequate vitamins and minerals enables the body to function at optimum energy levels throughout the morning. A good breakfast helps reduce the typical midmorning tiredness and the need for coffee. Circadian rhythms or sleep patterns are unbalanced in people who regularly skip breakfast. This often leads to eating late at night.

"Children with access to a SBP [school breakfast program] consume fewer calories from fat and are less likely to have low serum levels of vitamin C, vitamin E, and folate. They are also more likely to meet recommendations for the intake of fiber, potassium, and iron."[8]

An increasing number of studies are showing the necessity of getting more fruits and vegetables daily. One of them, from the Harvard School of Public Health stated,

> The largest and longest study to date, done as part of the Harvard-based Nurses' Health Study and Health Professionals Follow-up Study, included almost 110,000 men and women whose health and dietary habits were followed for 14 years. The higher the average daily intake of fruits and vegetables, the lower the chances of developing cardiovascular disease. Compared with those in the lowest category of fruit and vegetable intake (less than 1.5 servings a day), those who averaged 8 or more servings a day were 30 percent less likely to have had a heart attack or stroke. Although all fruits and vegetables likely contribute to this benefit [reduced coronary heart disease], green leafy vegetables such as lettuce, spinach, Swiss chard, and mustard greens; cruciferous vegetables such as broccoli, cauliflower, cabbage, Brussels sprouts, bok choy, and kale; and citrus fruits such as oranges, lemons, limes, and grapefruit (and their juices) make important contributions.

> When researchers combined findings from the Harvard studies with several other long-term studies in the U.S. and Europe, and looked at coronary heart disease and stroke separately, they found a similar protective effect: Individuals who ate more than 5 servings of fruits and vegetables per day had roughly a 20 percent lower risk of coronary heart disease and stroke, compared with individuals who ate less than 3 servings per day.[9]

The process of reviewing a significant number of studies to look for trends is called a meta-analysis. A meta-analysis of studies on the increased consumption of fruit and vegetables also revealed a reduced risk of coronary heart disease.[10]

Breakfast provides the opportunity to eat fruit and fruit juice, part of the needed daily servings of fruits and vegetables.

Eating breakfast improves concentration and performance on the job or in the classroom.

A nutritious breakfast includes fruits, grains, nuts, and soymilk or nutmilk.

5. WHY DOES EATING A GOOD BREAKFAST IMPROVE OUR CONCENTRATION AND JOB PERFORMANCE?

Workers who eat a good breakfast have better attitudes toward their work and greater efficiency. Start your day with a positive approach. *Eat a good breakfast.* You will feel more energized and more positive. If you rush off to school or work without eating a good breakfast, you are likely to have much less energy, have greater fatigue, and be less positive about life in general. Studies have shown that eating a good breakfast helps children to have increased attention spans and perform better at school. They also enjoy better health.

The Sodexo Foundation commissioned a comprehensive study titled "Impact of School Breakfast on Children's Health and Learning: An Analysis of the Scientific Research." The executive summary stated,

> While no single study necessarily provides a uniquely definitive assessment of the SBP's [school breakfast program] benefits, and while some studies occasionally reach differing conclusions, the combined and quite consistent message of this body of research is that serving breakfast to those schoolchildren who don't get it elsewhere significantly improves their cognitive or mental abilities, enabling them to be more alert, pay better attention, and to do better in terms of reading, math and other standardized test scores. Children who eat breakfast also are sick less often, have fewer problems associated with hunger, such as dizziness, lethargy, stomachaches and earaches, and do significantly better than their non-breakfasted peers in terms of cooperation, discipline and inter-personal behaviors.[11]

The evidence is clear. If we want our children to do their best, it is important to send them off to school with a substantial nutritious breakfast. By spending a little more time fixing a good breakfast for our family, we are likely to spend less time on behavioral problems.

Breakfast provides an excellent source of fiber.

6. WHAT FOODS CONTAIN THE MOST DIETARY FIBER?

A. _____

B. _____

C. _____

Dietary fiber is found in fresh fruits and vegetables, whole grains, beans, and other natural products. Fiber is the portion from the plant material we eat that cannot be digested by the enzymes of our gastrointestinal tract. It is essential to eat an abundance of fruits, nuts, grains, and vegetables to maintain good health and get adequate amounts of fiber in the diet.

According to the Harvard School of Public Health, most American diets are deficient in dietary fiber. "The average American eats only 15 grams of fiber" daily when they should be getting at least 30 grams daily.[12] William E. Wheeler states that "fiber is the number one nutrient that is deficient in most American diets."[13] A high-fiber diet aids in digestion, helps control our weight, benefits the heart, and reduces the risk of bowel cancer. It is found in abundance in wholesome, natural plant-based foods, especially legumes.

(For additional material on fiber, see page 41 in the *Natural Lifestyle Cooking* cookbook.)

Modern medical researchers have concluded that dietary fiber aids in reducing the risk of both heart disease and cancer. Dietary fiber is essential to good health.

EATING A GOOD BREAKFAST AIDS THE DIGESTIVE SYSTEM

Eating a good breakfast and digestion are related. When we wake up in the morning, we usually have not eaten for ten to twelve hours. Our glucose or blood-sugar level is at its lowest point in the day, and glucose is the basic fuel for the brain and central nervous system. A good breakfast starts our day off by supplying the body's basic fuel needs. It will keep us from being

Add some beans to your breakfast. They are high in fiber, nutritious, delicious, and satisfying.

tired and irritable by midmorning. Because the stomach is rested, there are two advantages related to digestion in eating a large, healthy nutritious breakfast.

1. All previous meals are well digested, and the stomach is ready to receive more food.

2. Digestive juices secreted by the stomach when we awake prepare our bodies to thoroughly digest our food.

In our classes on nutrition, a question is often asked: What about the traditional breakfast of coffee, doughnuts, bacon, and eggs?

EFFECT OF COFFEE ON THE DIGESTIVE SYSTEM

Caffeinated beverages are common in our culture. *Caffeine is the most widely used legal drug in the world.* The largest consumption of caffeine comes from coffee. For many people, coffee is the world's most enjoyable addiction. It is probably the world's most consumed beverage. In Western societies, many people start drinking coffee in their teens. However, there are some significant health risks associated with caffeinated beverages. It is very easy to develop a dependency on caffeine. In *Family Medical Guide,* Mervyn G. Hardinge and Harold Shryock discuss the detrimental effects of caffeine.

7. CAFFEINE'S DETRIMENTAL EFFECTS ARE:

   A. _____

"As larger amounts of caffeine are taken, the person becomes nervous, fidgety, irritable, develops tremors, and cannot sleep."[14]

   B. _____

"The risk of coronary heart attack is greatly increased in those drinking six or more cups of coffee a day. Chronic coffee users show elevated levels of blood cholesterol, blood fats (triglycerides), and blood sugar."[15]

"Even moderate doses of coffee increase the flow of both stomach acid (hydrochloric acid) and the protein-digesting enzyme, pepsin. The effect of decaffeinated coffee is only slightly less. Both caffeine-containing beverages and decaffeinated coffee produce digestive disturbances and heartburn, and either contribute to the initiation of ulcers or aggravate those already present."[16]

   C. _____

"Caffeine has a profound effect on the brain's higher functions. One to two cups of coffee will provide a feeling of well-being or euphoria (less fatigue), relief from drowsiness, and a more rapid flow of thought. It is this 'high' that makes the substance addictive, the so-called 'caffeine habit.' "[17]

Aileen Ludington and Hans Diehl, in *Health Power*, summarize the effects of caffeine use:

"Caffeine can produce:

- Elevated blood sugar

- Increased blood pressure

- Elevated blood fats (triglycerides)

- Heightened symptoms of PMS [premenstrual syndrome]

- Tremors, irritability, and nervousness

- Aggravation of anxiety disorders and panic attacks

- Increased stomach acid secretions

- Urinary calcium and magnesium losses

- Insomnia

- Irregular heart-beat

- Increased stimulation of the central nervous system. It overrules the need for rest."[18]

LONG-TERM EFFECTS OF MATERNAL CAFFEINE CONSUMPTION ON THE UNBORN CHILD

It is wise to carefully consider the effects of caffeine on fetal and neonatal development. Let's look at what selected international specialists have reported in research about the effects of a mother's use of caffeine on her unborn child.

Tetsuo Nakamoto summarizes scientific studies about the effects of caffeine on the unborn:

Caffeine's effects seem to be far-reaching, even beginning before fertilization. Premating caffeine ingestion (2.5 mg/100 g BW) for 130 days and during pregnancy caused an additional decrease of fetal cerebrum weight as well as decreased placental weight compared to a group that received caffeine during pregnancy alone . . . , suggesting that habitual caffeine intake before pregnancy might influence the future health of fetuses.

In humans, maternal ingestion of two cups of coffee during the last trimester decreases placental blood supply . . . , and perinatologic risks may be present.[19]

Nakamoto continues with the following:

Recently, we have shown that caffeine exposure during pregnancy caused a change in angiotensin II type 2 receptor gene expression in the placenta of pregnant rats that were fed a diet supplemented with caffeine, suggesting that caffeine intake alters gene expression of the developing organ in the early stages of life. This alteration may cause certain diseases that we are not aware of at the present time in the later life of the offspring. . . . Chronic caffeine exposure for human fetal neurodevelopment during the critical growth period could result in disease and modified behavior in later life, as it does in animal studies. . . . Thus, it may be critical to assess the early effect of caffeine in later life. . . .

I propose that serious consideration be given to the concept of the interrelationship of caffeine consumption, fetal and neonatal development, and possible disease development in the later years. Many diseases in the later years of human life are believed to originate in early fetal life. . . . If this is so, it would not be surprising to learn that caffeine exposure in early life is responsible for various diseases and/or behaviors we are currently not aware of. In fact, the increased susceptibility to gastric lesions in later life has been demonstrated in animals exposed to caffeine during pregnancy . . . , and SIDS could possibly be related to heavy maternal caffeine consumption. . . . In general, numerous animal studies have shown permanent behavioral changes long after caffeine exposure had ended.

The Food and Drug Administration (FDA) has advised pregnant women to avoid caffeine-containing drinks. . . . Given evidence of the adverse effects of caffeine consumption, the FDA on an ongoing basis should strongly discourage the use of all caffeine-containing substances by pregnant or lactating women and by those who plan to have children until caffeine's effects on humans during these critical periods become further clarified.[20]

Neil Nedley, in his book *Proof Positive: How to Reliably Combat Disease and Achieve Optimal Health Through Nutrition and Lifestyle,* discusses the relationship between the use of coffee and bladder cancer:

Pancreas cancer has probably received the most attention regarding increased risk from coffee. This apparently derives in large part from a highly publicized Harvard study in the early 1980s. . . .

. . . Other research such as that conducted at the State University of New York at Buffalo has confirmed the potential of coffee drinking to double bladder cancer risk. . . .

Other studies have also shown an increase in bladder cancer with coffee usage or other caffeinated beverages. This has led some to speculate that for bladder cancer, caffeine itself may be the main culprit in coffee. Fatal colon cancer has also been linked to coffee consumption. Those consuming two or more cups of coffee per day increased their risk of death from colon cancer by 70 percent when compared to those that consumed less than one cup a day. The study also revealed a dose-response relationship; that is, the more coffee consumed the higher the risk.[21]

With all the information we have today on the detrimental effects of coffee on the brain and the relationship of caffeine and cancer, maybe we should consider the words of a prominent nineteenth-century health educator, who said, "Coffee is a hurtful indulgence. It temporarily excites the mind to unwonted action, but the aftereffect is exhaustion, prostration, paralysis

Natural cereal beverages are a healthful substitute for coffee.

of the mental, moral, and physical powers. The mind becomes enervated, and unless through determined effort the habit is overcome, the activity of the brain is permanently lessened."[22]

Drinking noncaffeinated cereal beverages or herbal teas rather than coffee is a step toward better health for you and your family. There are healthful options for coffee lovers. Try some of these noncaffeinated hot drinks. They are wonderful healthful options.

Americans fondness for including eggs as part of their breakfast menu is another major risk factor in the average high-fat, high-cholesterol diet. Researcher Dr. David Spence studied more than twelve hundred people and found that egg consumption accelerates atherosclerosis or the buildup of plague on the arteries. The yolk of a jumbo egg contains 237 mg of cholesterol. Dr. Spence describes it this way, "It's more than the cholesterol in a Hardee's monster thick burger which is two-thirds of a pound thick beef, three slices of cheese and four slices of bacon."[23] He claims that the yolk of an egg contains about all the cholesterol the human body can handle without developing fatty patches in the heart and brain arteries over the years.

Let's return to the question we raised at the beginning of this section. What about the traditional breakfast of coffee, doughnuts, bacon, and eggs? The evidence is in and it is strong. Coffee is extremely detrimental to our health. Sugar-laden doughnuts and cholesterol-laden bacon and eggs predispose us to disease. With so many more natural foods that are tasty and healthful available, it is far wiser to give up those foods that diminish our health.

WHAT ABOUT COMMERCIAL CEREALS?

Dr. Ira Shannon and his coworkers at the Veterans Administration Hospital in Houston, Texas, analyzed seventy-eight commercial breakfast cereals for their overall sugar content. To their amazement, they discovered that twenty-three of the cereals proved to be 10 to 25 percent sugar, while twenty-four of the seventy-eight were a whopping 25 to 50 percent sugar.[24] This is certainly a good reason to prepare your own healthful breakfast cereals. Whole-grain cereals provide protein, calcium, iron, trace minerals, B vitamins, vitamin E in the germ, and, of course, fiber in the bran.

However, some commercially prepared cereals on the market are healthy. If you do not have time to prepare your own breakfast cereals, then make the best choices you can. Cereals that are high in fiber and low in sugar are the best. The grams of fiber should be higher than the grams of sugar. Read labels. Here are some examples of a few better cereals and the very best ones.

RECOMMENDED COMMERCIAL CEREALS

- **FIBER ONE.** This cereal is very high in fiber. It has 28 grams in every one-cup serving and 0 grams of sugar.

- **ALL-BRAN.** One cup has 20 grams of fiber. The fiber content is high, but so is the sugar content. It has 12 grams of sugar. Eat sparingly and try to get most of your fiber requirement from natural foods without the sugar.

- **CHEERIOS.** A one-cup serving has only 3 grams of fiber and just 1 gram of sugar, which is much lower in sugar than most cereals. Cheerios are fine occasionally, but don't depend on them all the time because the fiber is low.

HIGHLY RECOMMENDED COMMERCIAL CEREALS

- **SHREDDED WHEAT, SPOON SIZE.** A one-cup serving contains 6 grams fiber and 0 grams of sugar.

- **SHREDDED WHEAT.** It contains 100 percent natural whole-grain wheat with no sodium, 0 grams sugar, and 6 grams of fiber in two biscuits. It also contains iron, thiamine, niacin, vitamin B_6, folic acid, phosphorus, magnesium, zinc, and copper.

Here is a very tasty way of fixing Shredded Wheat and getting the added benefit of flaxseed.

SHREDDED WHEAT is a nutritious breakfast cereal.

Shredded Wheat

¾ c. boiling water
2 Shredded Wheat biscuits
1 t. honey

1 T. flaxseed, ground
Soymilk to taste (approximately 1 c.)

POUR ¾ cup boiling water over the Shredded Wheat biscuits. ADD honey, flaxseed, and soymilk.

Golden and brown flaxseed is high in omega-3.

Flaxseed has gained a reputation as a food extremely beneficial to our overall health. It contains potassium and phosphorus. *Flaxseed is rich in ALA (alpha-linolenic acid), which is a type of omega-3 fatty acid.*[25] Each tablespoon of ground flaxseed contains about 1.8 grams of omega-3s. Some studies suggest that omega-3 fatty acids may help reduce heart disease. Other preliminary studies show that flaxseed may be preventive against diabetes and breast cancer. Flaxseed also contains fiber. Try the BLUEBERRY PANCAKES recipe using flaxseed on page 52 of the *Natural Lifestyle Cooking* cookbook. My husband and I regularly eat blueberry pancakes for breakfast. These delicious pancakes are one of our family's favorite breakfasts.

Try **BLUEBERRY FLAXSEED PANCAKES**. You will love them!

EATING A HEALTHY BREAKFAST

Eating breakfast is one aspect of maintaining good health. Here are some guidelines that will ensure that our breakfasts give us optimum nutrition.

8. **LIST THE GUIDELINES FOR EATING A GOOD, HEALTHY BREAKFAST:**

A. _____

B. _____

C. _____

D. _____

E. _____

F. _____

Eating three to four servings of fresh fruit, two to four servings of whole grains, a handful of nuts and seeds, and fortified soymilk or nutmilk will certainly provide you with a good nutritious breakfast. Serving fresh fruit will make your breakfast not only healthful but also colorful. Serving food in an attractive way makes it much more appetizing. Have you ever noticed how much more you desire to eat something if it is served beautifully? Of course if the food doesn't taste good, serving it in an attractive way won't motivate your family to eat it. How a dish tastes is extremely important.

Choose recipes you think your family will enjoy. Healthy food does not need to be insipid, bland, and tasteless. The recipes in the *Natural Lifestyle Cooking* cookbook are delicious, simple, and easy. That makes it possible to serve your family a good, substantial breakfast. Be sure to budget enough time for breakfast to make it relaxing and enjoyable. Set the table the night before, if necessary. If you are making the oatmeal, blueberry, or whole-wheat pancakes, you can even mix all the dry ingredients ahead of time and add the liquid in the morning just before cooking the pancakes. We often set the table and prepare nonperishables ahead to make the preparation easier in the morning. Why not try preparing breakfast ahead of time as much as possible. Your morning breakfast preparation will go more smoothly.

FOODS TO EAT FOR A HEALTHY BREAKFAST

9. **WHAT FOOD GROUPS COMPRISE A HEALTHY BREAKFAST?**

   A. _____

   B. _____

   C. _____

   D. _____

   E. _____

Getting an adequate amount of fresh fruit and whole grains is necessary for good health. Start your day off right by eating a nutritious breakfast. We can certainly add extra protein to our diet by eating nuts, legumes, and soymilk or nutmilk at breakfast time. Try the **BREAKFAST BEAN** recipe on page 59 in the *Natural Lifestyle Cooking* cookbook. Many people are surprised at how tasty they really are.

CASHEW-OAT WAFFLES are really tasty!
You can find them on page 54 of the *Natural Lifestyle Cooking* cookbook.

ADDITIONAL RECIPES TO GIVE VARIETY TO YOUR BREAKFAST MENU

We've included additional breakfast recipes in this workbook for you to try to help add variety to your breakfast menus.

GEMS: Gems are a kind of unleavened flatbread. They will put a little more variety in your breakfast. You can make the gems ahead of time and make the gravy in the morning.

Unleavened Gems

1 ¼ c. whole-wheat flour
1 ¼ c. unbleached enriched flour
½ t. salt

1 c. water
⅓ c. light olive oil

In a medium-size bowl, COMBINE flour and salt. ADD oil slowly while mixing. ADD water and MIX well until smooth. ADD a little more flour if sticky. SHAPE biscuits small and quite flat. BAKE at 375°F for 10 minutes. REDUCE heat to 275°F for 30 minutes or until baked through. NOTE: Gems can be broken and placed in a bowl with **"CHICKEN" GRAVY** poured over them.

"Chicken" Gravy

⅓ c. light olive oil
½ c. unbleached enriched flour
3 to 4 c. water

1 t. Bragg's® Liquid Aminos
1 ½ T. McKay's® chicken seasoning

In a saucepan, MIX oil and flour until smooth. ADD water and Bragg's Liquid Aminos. BRING to a boil. COOK until thick, STIRRING constantly. ADD chicken seasoning. POUR over unleavened gems. NOTE: For thicker gravy, use 3 cups of water.

Gems and gravy may be new to you, but give them a try.

WHOLE-WHEAT BANANA PANCAKES are one of my favorites.

Whole-Wheat Banana Pancakes

2 c. whole-wheat flour

2 T. ground flaxseed

1 ½ t. salt

2 ¼ t. Rumford® baking powder

⅓ c. chopped walnuts

2 c. soymilk

2 T. light olive oil

¼ c. honey

2 mashed bananas

COMBINE all dry ingredients. ADD liquid ingredients and mashed bananas. POUR onto griddle from ¼ cup measuring cup. COOK on both sides. NOTE: Makes approximately 15 pancakes.

MILLET: Millet is a very nutritious but uncommonly used grain. It is unusual in that it is alkaline forming rather than acidic forming. Millet will be a positive, healthful addition to your diet, so here is a tasty millet recipe for breakfast. Serve the millet with some **STRAWBERRY APPLESAUCE** and **STRAWBERRY JAM** on homemade raisin bread along with your favorite fresh fruit. You will be nutritionally satisfied.

Millet is an alkaline-forming grain.
It is important to include in our diet more alkaline-forming foods than acidic-forming foods.

Nutritious Millet

2 c. water
1 c. soymilk
3/4 t. salt
1 t. vanilla

1/2 c. dates, chopped
1/2 c. coconut
1 c. millet
1/2 c. chopped walnuts (optional)

COMBINE water, soymilk, salt, vanilla, dates, and coconut. BRING to a boil, and ADD millet. SIMMER about 40 to 45 minutes. TOP with walnuts.

I'm sure you have heard that old saying, "An apple a day keeps the doctor away." Well, it's true that apples are good for you. STRAWBERRY APPLESAUCE is a delicious way to serve apples to your family.

Strawberry Applesauce

4 c. applesauce
1 c. frozen strawberries with juice
1 c. fresh strawberries

MIX strawberries with applesauce. SERVE.

STRAWBERRY APPLESAUCE is one of my husband's favorites.

Enjoy some delicious **STRAWBERRY JAM** on your homemade raisin bread!

Strawberry Jam

3 c. strawberries

1/4 c. dried mangoes

1 c. frozen white grape juice concentrate

1/4 c. honey or 100 percent pure maple syrup

1/2 c. water

1/4 c. cornstarch

BLEND strawberries and mangoes. POUR into saucepan. ADD grape juice concentrate and honey. MIX water and cornstarch and ADD to strawberry mixture. SIMMER until mixture is thick.

Note: There are many delicious, healthy breakfast options in the *Natural Lifestyle Cooking* cookbook on pages 39–60. Although some of these breakfast recipes may be new to you, try them. And remember, they contain the essential nutrients for good health.

Upon awakening in the morning, why not practice this simple routine?

• Begin your day by thanking God for another new day of life.

• Read a verse from the Bible.

• Drink one or two glasses of warm water.

• Take a twenty- to thirty-minute walk.

• Eat a good breakfast.

Although this routine may require getting up a little earlier, the rewards will be good health, a positive mental attitude, and a closer walk with God. It will be well worth it.

1.   A. Feel too rushed; no time
     B. Inconvenient
     C. Feel too tired
     D. Not hungry
     E. Desire to lose weight

2.   A. Detrimental effects of skipping breakfast on children
        i. Lowered attention span
        ii. Poorer classroom attitudes
     B. Benefits of eating a good breakfast
        i. Increased attention span
        ii. Positive classroom attitudes
        iii. Greater learning ability

3.   A. Help us concentrate better
     B. Give us more strength
     C. Help us maintain a healthy weight

4.   Because our body's energy needs must be satisfied early, or we will experience midmorning fatigue.

5.   A good breakfast supplies the vitamins and minerals the body needs for maximum performance. The B-complex vitamins especially increase our mental alertness.

6.   A. Fresh fruits and vegetables
     B. Whole grains
     C. Beans

7.   A. Associated with nervousness, anxiety, and muscular tremors
     B. Associated with stomach ulcers and increased rates of heart disease
     C. An addictive stimulant

8.   A. Nutritious
     B. Delicious
     C. Attractive
     D. Colorful
     E. Simple and easy
     F. Relaxing

9.   A. Fresh fruit
     B. Whole grains
     C. Legumes
     D. Nuts
     E. Soymilk or nutmilk

ENDNOTES

1. American News Service, "Seven Secrets to a Long Life," Berkshire Publishing, February 17, 2000, accessed April 23, 2013, http://www.berkshirepublishing.com/ans/HTMView.asp?parItem=S031000342A.

2. "Poor Breakfast Habits Could Be Affecting America's Health," *Rome (Ga.) News Tribune,* January 24, 2005, accessed April 23, 2013, http://news.google.com/newspapers?nid=348&dat=20050124&id=jBwuAAAAIBAJ&sjid=PjwDAAAAIBAJ&pg=7127,472816.

3. "Breakfast Basics for Busy Families," Eat Right, accessed April 23, 3013, http://www.eatright.org/Public/content.aspx?id=6442460400.

4. PR Newswire, "Survey Reveals Dismal State of the American Breakfast; Poor Breakfast Habits Could Be Affecting Americans Health," PR Newswire, January 5, 2005, accessed July 8, 2013, http://www.prnewswire.com/news-releases/survey-reveals-dismal-state-of-the-american-breakfast-53860442.html.

5.   Ibid.

6.   Frances Goulart, "First Things First: 22 Ways to Build a Better Breakfast," *Vegetarian Times* 63 (November 1982): 51. See also "School Breakfast Participation Leads to Academic, Psychosocial Improvements," KidSource Online, accessed July 8, 2013, http://www.kidsource.com/kidsource/content4/school.breakfast.part.html.

7.   Kathleen M. Zelman, "The Many Benefits of Breakfast," WebMD, accessed July 8, 2013, http://www.webmd.com/diet/features/many-benefits-breakfast.

8.   J. Bhattacharya, J. Currie, and S. Hadler, "Breakfast of Champions? The School Breakfast Program and Nutrition of Children and Families," *Journal of Human Resources* 41, no. 3 (Summer 2006): 445–466.

9.   Harvard University School of Public Health, "Vegetables and Fruits: Get Plenty Every," The Nutrition Source, accessed April 23, 2013, http://www.hsph.harvard.edu/nutritionsource/vegetables-full-story/.

10.   F. J. He et al., "Increased Consumption of Fruit and Vegetables Is Related to a Reduced Risk of Coronary Heart Disease: Meta-analysis of Cohort Studies," *Journal of Human Hypertension* 21 (2007): 717–728.

11.   J. Larry Brown, William H. Beardslee, and Deborah Prothrow-Stith, "Impact of School Breakfast on Children's Health and Learning: An Analysis of the Scientific Research," Sodexo Foundation, accessed April 23, 2012, http://www.sodexofoundation.org/hunger_us/Images/Impact%20of%20School%20Breakfast%20Study_tcm150-212606.pdf.

12.   Harvard University School of Public Health, "Fiber: Start Roughing It!" The Nutrition Source, accessed March 23, 2013, http://www.hsph.harvard.edu/nutritionsource/fiber-full-story/.

13.   William E. Wheeler, quoted in Wyatt Myers, "The Benefits of a High-Fiber Diet," Everyday Health, accessed April 17, 2013, http://www.everydayhealth.com/health-report/healthy-eating/benefits-of-a-high-fiber-diet.aspx.

14.   Mervyn G. Hardinge and Harold Shryock, *Family Medical Guide,* rev. ed. (Nampa, Idaho: Pacific Press® Publishing Association, 1994), 1:262.

15.   Ibid.

16.   Ibid.

17.   Ibid., 261..

18.   Aileen Ludington and Hans Diehl, *Health Power* (Hagerstown, Md.: Review and Herald® Publishing Association, 2005), 77.

19.   Tetsuo Nakamoto, "Neurodevelopmental Consequences of Coffee/Caffeine Exposure," in *Coffee, Tea, Chocolate, and the Brain,* ed. Astrid Nehlig, Nutrition, Brain, and Behavior (Boca Raton, Fla.: CRC Press 2004), 101.

20.   Ibid., 107, 108.

21.   Neil Nedley, *Proof Positive* (Ardmore, Okla.: Nedley Publications, 1999), 30, 31.

22.   Ellen G. White, *Counsels on Diet and Foods* (Hagerstown, Md.: Review and Herald®, 2001), 421.

23.   CBC News, "Egg Yolks Almost as Dangerous as Smoking, Researcher Says," CBC News, accessed July 8, 2013, http://www.cbc.ca/news/canada/sudbury/story/2012/08/14/wdr-egg-yolk.html.

24.   Jean Mayer, "Candy Masks as Cereal," *Lakeland (Fla.) Ledger,* December 3, 1975, 4C, accessed July 8, 2013, http://news.google.com/newspapers?id=voosAAAAIBAJ&sjid=4foDAAAAIBAJ&pg=6877%2C504621.

25.   Harvard University School of Public Health, "Ask the Expert: Omega-3 Fatty Acids," The Nutrition Source, accessed April 23, 2013, http://www.hsph.harvard.edu/nutritionsource/omega-3/.

Class 3

Planning a Balanced Menu

Meal Balancing · Economy

Health is a hot topic today. People around the world are concerned about their well-being. They are also becoming increasingly concerned about what to eat to experience optimum health. The *scientific evidence* that *confirms the benefits of a plant-based diet is gaining worldwide acceptance.* However, many people are still concerned about just how to prepare balanced meals. *Careful planning* is vitally important to achieve *a well-balanced diet.* As you take time to prepare well-balanced meals, your efforts will pay rich dividends. You will be rewarded bountifully. Your family's meals will have greater variety, contain more health-giving nutrients, be more enjoyable, and be much more economical.

During this session, "Planning a Balanced Menu," we will explore the *benefits of a plant-based diet* consisting of a wide variety of fruits, nuts, seeds, grains, and vegetables. We will also discover how to prepare *nutritious, well-balanced meals* that are both *tasty and economical.*

People around the world are increasingly suffering from chronic diseases. Recent research reveals the importance of diet in reducing the risk of these lifestyle diseases causing premature death. Eating healthier will help reduce your risk of these diseases.

Planning a balanced menu on a plant-based diet

1. WHAT ARE CHRONIC DISEASES?

2. WHAT ROLE DOES DIET PLAY IN THESE DISEASES?

"Chronic diseases are diseases of long duration and generally slow progression. Chronic diseases, such as heart disease, stroke, cancer, chronic respiratory diseases and diabetes, are by far the leading cause of mortality in the world, representing 63% of all deaths. Out of the 36 million people who died from chronic disease in 2008, nine million were under 60 and ninety per cent of these premature deaths occurred in low- and middle-income countries."[1]

Because *diet is a main factor in reducing chronic diseases,* how can we prepare better meals for our families? Is there a *plan to balance our meals* that will help us know exactly what we should eat to stay healthy?

We will start by taking a brief look at the *history of the guidelines established by the United States Department of Agriculture* (USDA) on nutrition and meal balancing.

The *USDA's first nutrition guidelines were published in 1894* by Dr. Wilbur Olin Atwater as a farmers' bulletin. In a later edition in 1904, titled *Principles of Nutrition and Nutritive Value of Food,*[2] Dr. Atwater advocated variety, proportionality, and moderation; measuring calories; and an efficient, affordable diet that focused on nutrient-rich foods and less fat, sugar, and starch. This information preceded the discovery of individual vitamins in 1910.

A new guide in 1916, named *Food for Young Children* by nutritionist Caroline Hunt, categorized foods into *five groups: dairy and meat; cereals; vegetables and fruits; fats and fatty foods; and sugars and sugary foods.* Throughout the twentieth century, continuing research and dietary studies revealed the need for revision of the original recommendations.

The USDA's "Basic 7" food groups from 1943 to 1956

From 1943 to 1956, the USDA promoted the "Basic 7" food groups.

The "Basic 7" food groups were later reclassified. From 1956 until 1992, the United States Department of Agriculture recommended its "Basic 4" food groups.

CATEGORIES INCLUDED IN "BASIC 4"

- VEGETABLES AND FRUITS
- MILK
- MEAT
- CEREALS AND BREADS

3. **WHAT WERE THE FOUR CATEGORIES INCLUDED IN THE "BASIC 4" FROM 1956 TO 1992?**

A. _____

B. _____

C. _____

D. _____

In 1992, the USDA introduced the Food Guide Pyramid. This guide to meal balancing and adequate nutrition took a different approach. For the first time it listed the nutritional value of the food groups in order of their priority, with the most important at the base of the pyramid and the least important at the top. The Food Guide Pyramid was used widely for nutrition education in the United States.

FOOD GUIDE PYRAMID

The introduction of the USDA's Food Guide Pyramid in 1992 attempted to express the recommended servings of each food group, which previous guides did not do. It included

The USDA's 1992 Food Guide Pyramid

- **SIX TO ELEVEN SERVINGS OF BREAD, CEREAL, RICE, AND PASTA,** which occupied the large base of the pyramid
- **THREE TO FIVE SERVINGS OF VEGETABLES**
- **TWO TO FOUR SERVINGS OF FRUIT**
- **TWO TO THREE SERVINGS OF MILK, YOGURT, AND CHEESE**
- **TWO TO THREE SERVINGS OF MEAT, POULTRY, FISH, DRY BEANS, EGGS, AND NUTS**
- **USED SPARINGLY—FATS, OILS, AND SWEETS**

Within each group there were several images of different types of foods. There were also symbols representing the fat and sugar contents of the foods.

From 1992 onward, this guide on foods was a mainstay of nutrition education in the United States and was considered almost the definitive word on nutrition by the vast majority of Americans. The Food Guide Pyramid pictures fruits, vegetables, and grains at its broad base, emphasizing the nutritional importance of these foods. The pyramid pictures meat and dairy products at the upper, smaller portion of the pyramid, just below oils, sweets, and fats. This particular guide promotes daily consumption of two to three servings from the meat and dairy groups.

In 1992, the Physicians Committee for Responsible Medicine (PCRM), a health/nutrition advocacy group composed primarily of health professionals, challenged the government recommendations in the Food Guide Pyramid. They unveiled the New Four Food Groups plan. The PCRM argued, using recent scientific studies, that the previous emphasis of the "Basic 4" food groups and the Food Guide Pyramid on animal products, with their high amounts of fat, cholesterol, and protein, were a significant factor in degenerative diseases, such as heart disease, stroke, several types of cancer, and osteoporosis.[3]

THE NEW FOUR FOOD GROUPS

The PCRM recommended the following revised nutrition guide:[4]

1. THE WHOLE-GRAIN GROUP—5 or more servings a day, which includes bread, pasta, breakfast cereal, rice dishes, corn, and other grains. The grain group provides fiber, complex carbohydrates, important vitamins, and an adequate amount of protein. Especially valuable are unprocessed whole-grain products, as compared to grains that have been ground up into flour or stripped of their bran.

2. THE VEGETABLE GROUP—4 or more servings a day, which includes such items as broccoli, carrots, lettuce, cabbage, potatoes, and cauliflower. Vegetables are particularly rich in vitamins and minerals. Beta carotene, found primarily in yellow and green vegetables, such as carrots, broccoli, and spinach, reduces the risk of cancer and other diseases. Green leafy vegetables are also very good sources of fiber, complex carbohydrates, and calcium.

3. THE FRUIT GROUP—3 or more servings a day, which includes such items as apples, bananas, peaches, pears, and oranges as well as exotic fruits, such as kiwis. Fruits are very rich in complex carbohydrates, vitamins, and fiber; they provide valuable resistance to heart disease, cancer, and other degenerative diseases.

4. THE LEGUME GROUP—2 or more servings a day, which includes foods that come in a pod, such as beans, peas, lentils, and foods produced from legumes, such as tofu. These foods are excellent sources of fiber, complex carbohydrates, protein, and minerals.

In addition to providing all the necessary nutrients for good health, the New Four Food Groups contain no cholesterol and, with a few exceptions, such as nuts and avocados, is very low in fat. However, nuts and avocados are good nutritious natural fats. The low fat content of these foods make them especially valuable in sensible long-term weight-control programs.

The New Four Food Groups was presented by Neal Barnard, director of the Physicians Committee of Responsible Medicine. Dr. Barnard asserted that the new proposal could have a major impact on diet-related diseases in the U.S. He added that the old "Basic 4," which involves meat and other animal products at the center of the American diet, is a recipe for serious health problems.

On January 31, 1995, the PCRM submitted its "Recommended Revisions for Dietary Guidelines for Americans." The PCRM analysis stated that the government's current review process was an excellent time to take advantage of recent research findings "that indicate the enormous potential of dietary factors to reduce the risk of serious illness and premature mortality." They emphasized the value of a shift from the current recommendations, which included animal products as a substantial part of the diet, to recommendations based on plant-centered nutrition.[5]

In 2005, the USDA updated its guide with MyPyramid, which replaced the Food Guide Pyramid with colorful vertical wedges, often displayed without images of foods, creating a more abstract design. Stairs were added up the left side of the pyramid with an icon of someone climbing them to represent exercise.

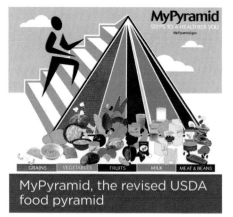
MyPyramid, the revised USDA food pyramid

4. WHAT IS THE NEWEST NUTRITIONAL GUIDE ON MEAL BALANCING BY THE UNITED STATES DEPARTMENT OF AGRICULTURE (USDA)?

THE MYPLATE NUTRITION GUIDE

MyPlate is the current nutrition guide published by the United States Department of Agriculture, consisting of a diagram of a plate divided into four food groups with a small circle on the side for the dairy group. The aim of MyPlate is to help people know how to balance their diets. After nineteen years of use, the MyPyramid diagram was replaced with the MyPlate diagram in January 2011. The guide has since been displayed on food packaging and used in nutritional education in the United States.

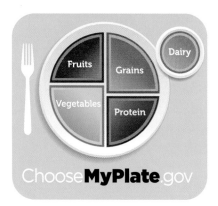

Our daughter Rebecca is a registered dietitian. Recently, in the process of renewing her dietitian's license, she made a game for children on the MyPlate Nutrition Guide as one of her projects. On a visit to an educational museum with our grandchildren, we noticed that one entire section was also devoted to nutrition with a MyPlate replica made with plastic foods. These are great ways for children to learn the various food groups and what foods are best for them.

The USDA MyPlate concept is simple and easy. It is a brightly colored visual plate, which makes it a lot easier for people to remember than the previous charts. It is certainly much less confusing than the food pyramid. The USDA felt this was a great improvement over the food pyramid. The basic goals of MyPlate are to teach people how to do the following:

- **BALANCE CALORIES** (reduce portions)

- **INCREASE CONSUMPTION OF CERTAIN FOODS** (vegetables, fruits, and whole grains)

- **REDUCE CONSUMPTION OF OTHER FOODS** (high-sodium foods and sugary drinks)

The round USDA plate is divided into four sections with another section—a small circle—beside the plate. This easy-to-read MyPlate graphic is designed to do the following:

- **PRESENT** the four basic food groups in a visually attractive color-coded plate.
- **MOTIVATE** us to increase our intake of fruits and vegetables.
- **PROVIDE** us with an eating guide for good nutrition.
- **DESCRIBE** the servings of vegetables, fruits, grains, and proteins we need daily.
- **ASSIST** us in reducing the intake of proteins, especially fatty meats.

A smaller circle next to the plate represents the daily serving of dairy. (We recommend replacing the dairy with plant-based dairy substitutes.)

Researchers at the Harvard School of Public Health say MyPlate is an improvement over the pyramid, but does not offer enough information about good nutrition. Therefore, in September 2011, Harvard University revealed a modified version of the USDA plate that would include specific information about what to eat and what to avoid and would make healthy recommendations.

5. WHAT IS THE NAME OF THE HARVARD UNIVERSITY-MODIFIED VERSION OF MYPLATE?

Harvard's "Healthy Eating Plate" has the same four sections that MyPlate has, but with more detailed information on what foods to eat, and which ones to avoid. Walter Willett, professor of epidemiology and nutrition at Harvard, says, "The main thing is that MyPlate isn't specific enough to really give enough guidance."[6] So let's take a look at the Healthy Eating Plate.

"The Harvard plate . . . is detailed in its recommendations, differentiating among foods in a given category and more importantly, it is explicit about foods not to eat," said Dr. David Katz, founding director of the Yale University Prevention Research Center.[7]

The Harvard Health Blog says, MyPlate "says nothing about the quality of carbohydrates (grains). White bread and white rice raises blood sugar in a flash—whole grains are better for long-term health."[8]

"In addition, MyPlate recommends milk or dairy at every meal, even though there is little evidence that high dairy intake protects against osteoporosis and substantial evidence that consuming a lot of milk and dairy foods can be harmful. It says nothing about healthy oils, which are good for the heart, arteries, and the rest of the body. And it is shockingly silent on sugary drinks, which provide far too many empty calories."[9] Now that the deficiencies of MyPlate have been noted, let's take a look at the Harvard University Healthy Eating Plate.

The Healthy Eating Plate was created by nutrition experts at the Harvard School of Public Health, in conjunction with Harvard Health Publications. They say the Healthy Eating Plate can be your blueprint for planning a healthy, balanced meal.

Here are some suggestions adapted from the Harvard Medical School that we would recommend:

HEALTHY EATING PLATE

- **"FILL HALF OF YOUR PLATE WITH VEGETABLES AND FRUITS.** The more color, and the more variety on this part of the plate, the better.

- **"SAVE A QUARTER OF YOUR PLATE FOR WHOLE GRAINS—NOT JUST ANY GRAINS:** Whole grains—whole wheat, brown rice, and foods made with them, such as whole-wheat pasta—have a gentler effect on blood sugar and insulin than white bread, white rice, and other so-called 'refined' grains." That's why the Healthy Eating Plate says to choose whole grains—the less processed, the better—and limited refined grains.

- **"PUT A HEALTHY SOURCE OF PROTEIN ON ONE QUARTER OF YOUR PLATE":** We recommend beans, nuts, and seeds because these contain beneficial nutrients, such as the heart-healthy omega-3 fatty acids and the fiber in beans. We would recommend that you avoid all animal products. The Harvard Healthy Eating Plate includes chicken and fish, but they do encourage us to "avoid processed meats—bacon, cold cuts, hot dogs, and the like—since over time, regularly eating even small amounts of these foods raises the risk of heart disease, type 2 diabetes, and colon cancer.

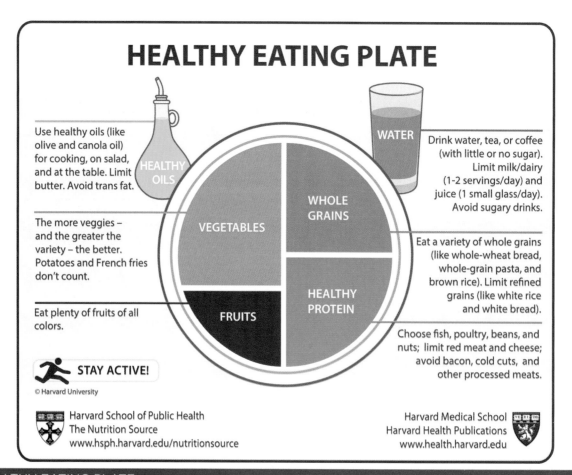

HEALTHY EATING PLATE

Use healthy oils (like olive and canola oil) for cooking, on salad, and at the table. Limit butter. Avoid trans fat.

HEALTHY OILS

VEGETABLES

WHOLE GRAINS

HEALTHY PROTEIN

FRUITS

WATER

Drink water, tea, or coffee (with little or no sugar). Limit milk/dairy (1-2 servings/day) and juice (1 small glass/day). Avoid sugary drinks.

The more veggies – and the greater the variety – the better. Potatoes and French fries don't count.

Eat a variety of whole grains (like whole-wheat bread, whole-grain pasta, and brown rice). Limit refined grains (like white rice and white bread).

Eat plenty of fruits of all colors.

Choose fish, poultry, beans, and nuts; limit red meat and cheese; avoid bacon, cold cuts, and other processed meats.

STAY ACTIVE!

© Harvard University

Harvard School of Public Health
The Nutrition Source
www.hsph.harvard.edu/nutritionsource

Harvard Medical School
Harvard Health Publications
www.health.harvard.edu

HEALTHY EATING PLATE
Copyright © 2011 Harvard University. For more information about The Healthy Eating Plate, please see The Nutrition Source, Department of Nutrition, Harvard School of Public Health, http://www.thenutritionsource.org and Harvard Health Publications, health.harvard.edu.

Complete healthy eating plate for dinner: **MILLET PATTIES**, red roasted potatoes, fresh salad, and broccoli.

- **"USE HEALTHY PLANT OILS.** The glass bottle near the Healthy Eating Plate is a reminder to use healthy vegetable oils, such as olive, canola, soy, corn, sunflower, peanut, and others, in cooking, on salad, and at the table." We would recommend using olive oil as much as possible.

- **DRINK WATER.** Drink plenty of water. The Harvard Medical School's Healthy Eating Plate advises people to limit milk and dairy products to one to two servings per day, because high intakes are associated with increased risk of prostate cancer and possibly ovarian cancer. We would recommend avoiding all animal products and all caffeinated beverages and drinking large amounts of water.

- **"STAY ACTIVE.** The small red figure running across the Healthy Eating Plate's placemat is a reminder that staying active is half of the secret to weight control. The other half is eating a healthy diet with modest portions that meet your calorie needs."[10]

Although the Healthy Eating Plate from Harvard is a great guide for eating balanced meals, I would like to suggest another plate. I call it the "Complete Healthy Eating Plate." It comes right from the Garden of Eden at the beginning of Creation, so it is a plant-based plate. Fruits, vegetables, grains, nuts and seeds, and legumes are the basic food groups that will keep us healthy and living longer. Basically, meals should be planned around these food groups. This was the original diet provided by our Creator.

Our loving Creator has given us an abundance of natural foods to sustain life and prolong health. After creating an amazing variety of fruits, nuts, grains, and vegetables, He declared, "You may freely eat" (Genesis 2:16).

Ellen White, a health educator in the 1800s, wrote, "In grains, fruits, vegetables, and nuts are to be found all the food elements that we need."[11]

6. WHAT ARE THE FOOD GROUPS GIVEN IN THE FIRST THREE CHAPTERS OF GENESIS THAT WILL KEEP US HEALTHY AND LIVING LONGER?

Of course, moderation is also an important part of health. Food is meant to be enjoyed. The healthier you eat, the more you will enjoy it—and the longer you will live to continue to enjoy it.

Plant-based foods are abundant in antioxidants. "Considerable laboratory evidence from chemical, cell culture, and animal studies indicates that antioxidants may slow or possibly prevent the development of cancer."[12]

ANTIOXIDANTS
Good food sources of antioxidants

- **VITAMIN C.** Citrus fruits and their juices, berries, dark-green vegetables (spinach, asparagus, green peppers, Brussels sprouts, broccoli, watercress, other greens), red and yellow bell peppers, tomatoes and tomato juice, pineapple, cantaloupe, mangoes, papaya, and guava.

Fruits, vegetables, grains, and nuts

- **VITAMIN E.** Vegetable oils such as olive, soybean, corn, cottonseed, and safflower; nuts and nut butters; seeds; whole grains; wheat; wheat germ; brown rice; oatmeal; soybeans; sweet potatoes; legumes (beans, lentils, split peas); and leafy dark-green vegetables.

- **SELENIUM.** Brazil nuts, brewer's yeast, oatmeal, brown rice, garlic, molasses, onions, wheat germ, whole grains, and most vegetables.

- **BETA CAROTENE.** Dark-orange, red, yellow, and green vegetables and fruits such as broccoli, kale, spinach, sweet potatoes, carrots, red and yellow bell peppers, apricots, cantaloupe, and mangoes.

An important step to help reduce the risk of chronic diseases is to eat plenty of antioxidant-rich foods. Antioxidants help protect your health by preventing and repairing damage caused to your cells by excessive free radicals.

According to a study published in the *Journal of Agricultural and Food Chemistry,* the following were the twenty most antioxidant-rich foods.[13]

MOST ANTIOXIDANT-RICH FOODS

Rank	Food	Serving Size	Antioxidant Capacity per Serving
1	Small red beans, dried	1/2 cup	13,727
2	Wild blueberries	1 cup	13,427
3	Red kidney beans, dried	1/2 cup	13,259
4	Pinto beans, dried	1/2 cup	11,864
5	Blueberries, cultivated	1 cup	9,019
6	Cranberries	1 cup	8,983
7	Artichoke hearts, cooked	1 cup	7,904
8	Blackberries	1 cup	7,701
9	Dried prunes	1/2 cup	7,291
10	Raspberries	1 cup	6,058
11	Strawberries	1 cup	5,938
12	Red Delicious apple	One	5,900
13	Granny Smith apple	One	5,381
14	Pecans	1 ounce	5,095
15	Sweet cherries	1 cup	4,873
16	Black plums	One	4,844
17	Russet potato, cooked	One	4,649
18	Black beans, dried	1/2 cup	4,181
19	Plums	One	4,118
20	Gala apple	One	3,903

Eat Foods With a Variety of Color

Notice all the color on the total vegetarian "shamburger" plate.
(The recipe for the **SHAMBURGER SANDWICH** is found on pages 69 and 111 in the *Natural Lifestyle Cooking* cookbook.)

7.   WHAT IS A SIMPLE PRINCIPLE IN GETTING A GOOD, NUTRITIOUS, WELL-BALANCED MEAL?

One very important guideline in getting a good, nutritious meal is being sure you include a variety of colors. Simply look at your plate at every meal. How colorful is it? You will notice that the *Natural Lifestyle Cooking* cookbook is filled with a variety of colors. Color is one of the most important things to think about in meal planning. The brighter and deeper the colors you have on your plate, the healthier your diet will be.

POINTS TO CONSIDER WHEN PLANNING MEALS

When planning healthy, balanced meals for your family, use some of these helpful hints:

- **MAKE YOUR MEALS COLORFUL.** An old saying states, "The more colorful your plate, the more balanced your meal."

- **USE FAMILY FAVORITES.** Although taste can be developed, learn what foods your family enjoys and find recipes that you know they will like. If meat is the mainstay you have been planning your meals around, begin to substitute a vegetarian protein dish that your family enjoys. Explore new, delightful ways of preparing fresh salads, colorful vegetable dishes, and plant-based proteins.

- **INCREASE USE OF FRESH PRODUCE.** Buy fruit and vegetables that are in season. Fruits and vegetables in season taste better, are less expensive, and are the most nutritious. Using locally grown fruits and vegetables is nutritionally beneficial because local produce retains more nutrients than does produce shipped over long distances, taking a long period of time before it reaches your table. Utilize farmers' markets and fruit stands to get greater nutrition, taste, and value.

- **INCLUDE FAMILY MEMBERS IN THE PREPARATION.** It can be enjoyable for various family members to take turns planning the menu and making the meals. You can start your children quite young in helping to prepare the family meals. Children love to get their hands in the dough and help Mama make homemade rolls or prepare healthy desserts.

- **PLAN VARIETY IN YOUR DIET.** Eating a wide variety of fruits, nuts, grains, vegetables, and legumes is the very best way to have a nutritious diet and live a longer, healthier, and happier life.

KEYS TO A HEALTHY, BALANCED DIET

8. **WHAT ARE THREE PRACTICAL KEYS TO A HEALTHY, BALANCED DIET?**

   A. _____

   B. _____

   C. _____

KEY 1. EAT THE RIGHT KIND OF FOOD. Eat foods that are filled with vitamins and minerals. Eat an abundance of fruits, vegetables, grains, and nuts. Reduce or even eliminate those foods that are just empty calories.

A Helpful Nutritional Guide

EAT DAILY

- Four to five servings of vegetables
- Four to five servings of fresh fruits
- Six to eight servings of whole grains
- Two servings of legumes
- Handful of nuts and seeds
- Moderate amount of soymilk, rice milk, or nut milk
- Small amount of fats—natural fats are best!

KEY 2. EAT THE RIGHT AMOUNT OF FOOD based on your metabolism and your activity. The amount of food you eat should be proportioned between the four basic food groups so you get adequate amounts from each of these basic food groups.

KEY 3. EAT AT THE RIGHT TIMES. Eating at the right time is one of the real keys to managing the obesity problem. Many people eat throughout the day. Getting this one habit under control may be the key to help you lose those pounds you would like to shed. Start your day by eating a substantial, hearty breakfast. Follow breakfast by eating a nutritious dinner in the middle of the day. Eat a light supper with nothing in between meals. This should significantly help you control your weight.

9. HOW MANY MEALS A DAY DO WE NEED TO ENSURE A BALANCED DIET?

If meals are well planned, balanced, and nutritious, it is possible to get all the nutrients needed in just two meals a day. However, for some people to maintain their ideal weight, they may need three meals a day. Not everyone is alike, so it is best to consult your physician if you have special medical needs. This is especially true for diabetics. But if you are generally in good health, here is a possible guide to balancing your meals.

BREAKFAST: INCLUDE

- One serving whole-grain cereal or main dish
- Three or four servings fresh fruits
- One or two pieces of whole-grain bread

DINNER: INCLUDE

- Protein food—legumes, nut dishes
- A starch such as potatoes or a potato exchange such as rice or whole-grain pasta
- Fresh salad (with at least three or four fresh vegetables)
- Cooked vegetable

SUPPER: ONLY ONE OF THE FOLLOWING:

- Fresh fruit and toast
- Juice or smoothie
- Soup and crackers
- Sandwich and fruit

A nineteenth-century health educator named Ellen White wrote, "After disposing of one meal, the digestive organs need rest. At least five or six hours should intervene between the meals; and most persons who give the plan a trial, will find that two meals a day are better than three. . . .

". . . If a third meal be eaten at all, it should be light, and several hours before going to bed."[14] "In most cases, two meals a day are preferable to three. Supper, when taken at an early hour, interferes with the digestion of the previous meal. When taken later, it is not itself digested before bedtime. Thus the stomach fails of securing proper rest. The sleep is disturbed, the brain and nerves are wearied, the appetite for breakfast is impaired, the whole system is unrefreshed, and is unready for the day's duties."[15]

Some people may do better on three meals than two, so decide what is best for you. "Some do best healthwise when eating three light meals, and when they are restricted to two, they feel the change severely."[16]

REGULAR MEALS—WITH NOTHING BETWEEN

Eating the right kind and right amount of food is important for good health. Regularity in eating is another vital aspect of healthy living. Dr. Neil Nedley, in his book *Proof Positive*, discusses a suspected link between the frequency of times people eat and colon cancer. "Meal frequency has been identified as a risk factor for colon cancer. A number of studies in different parts of the world demonstrate that eating meals more frequently lead to an increased risk of colon cancer. Dr. La Vecchia and colleagues in Milan Italy have published on this subject. Their group found that the risk of both colon and rectal cancer could be nearly doubled by eating more frequently, as tabulated" in the chart below.[17]

COLON CANCER AND MEAL FREQUENCY

Meals per day	Risk of Rectal Cancer	Risk of Colon Cancer
2 or less	1.0	1.0
3	1.7	1.4
4 or more	1.9	1.9

Some nutritionists and dietitians promote eating multiple meals each day, but this is not the best program to maintain optimum health. As early as 1890, health educator Ellen White advocated eating only two or at most three meals a day.

"Most people enjoy better health while eating two meals a day than three; others, under their existing circumstances, may require something to eat at suppertime; but this meal should be very light. Let no one think himself a criterion for all,—that every one must do exactly as he does."[18]

Additional Tips for Eating Healthy, Balanced Meals

Eating balanced meals is an important part in maintaining good health. The following tips for healthy eating can help us make better, more healthful choices. If you are already making good choices by eating a wide variety of fruits, nuts, grains, and vegetables in as natural a state as possible, continue on your journey of good health.

- Eat at least eight or nine servings of **FRUITS AND VEGETABLES** every day.

- Get plenty of **FIBER** by eating adequate amounts of whole grains.

- **CUT** down on **FAT** and **SUGAR.**

- Eat **LESS SALT.**

- Try **JUICING** at least occasionally.

- Eat the **RIGHT AMOUNT OF CALORIES** to maintain your ideal weight.

- **DRINK** plenty of **WATER.** Eight 8-ounce glasses daily are recommended. These recommendations, of course, may vary depending on your age and weight.

You can eat economically while still maintaining a well-balanced diet. In this next section we will share thirteen tips on cooking economically.

TIPS ON COOKING ECONOMCALLY
Cheaper by the dozen—in fact—a baker's dozen

1. **EDUCATE YOURSELF.** When you are aware of the nutritional advantages of various foods, you are more likely to choose the ones that will benefit your health the most.

2. **MAKE WISE CHOICES.** In order to make wise choices, it is important to plan well. Choosing the right kinds of food does the most to reduce your food costs. Making good food choices might even save you an expensive medical bill.

3. **PLAN MEALS AND KEEP THEM SIMPLE.** Planning menus rather than spontaneously deciding what you are going to eat not only saves on the food budget but also helps you eat more nutritiously.

4. **CUT OUT THE JUNK FOODS.** Evaluate how much money you are spending on junk foods, such as soft drinks, sweets, prepackaged meals, and processed foods. Limit or completely cut out these unhealthy foods. Soft drinks, for example, are basically sugar and chemicals. Getting rid of these junk foods eliminates those foods that are empty calories and very low in nutritive value. It is a good idea to cut down on the prepared and processed foods and eat what is called "live" food rather than "dead" food.

5. **EAT OUT LESS.** Eating out is generally quite expensive and often it is not that nutritious. If you do eat out, choose your restaurant and menu items wisely.

6. **PREPARE A GROCERY LIST.** Preparing a grocery list keeps you from impulse buying. Keep a list on the fridge. Note: There is an extensive grocery list included in the appendix for all the recipes in the *Natural Lifestyle Cooking* cookbook.

7. **WATCH FOR SALES.** Every grocery store has regular sales. Particularly watch for fresh produce when there is a buy-one-get-one-free offer. Buy in bulk and stock up on nonperishable items and frozen foods.

8. **CLIP COUPONS.** You can save significantly by clipping coupons from your local newspaper, magazines, and flyers.

9. **BUY IN BULK.** Stock up on the nonperishables such as dry beans, rice, seasonings, dried fruit, etc.

10. **BUY IN SEASON.** When produce is in season, it is much cheaper and has more nutritional value. Locate the nearest farmer's market, buy in bulk, and do some canning and freezing. My husband and I can 100 to 150 quarts of applesauce every year. When our children were growing up, we canned or froze about two thousand quarts of fruits and vegetables each year.

11. **INCLUDE HOMEMADE ITEMS.** Home-baked foods—such as bread, rolls, cereals, and desserts—are a good way to save on your food budget and at the same time provide your family with tasty, nutritious foods. Another benefit of making your own home-baked foods is that you don't use all the additives and preservatives found in almost all prepackaged foods. Check out the variety of breads, breakfast foods, entrées, and desserts that are included in the *Natural Lifestyle Cooking* cookbook.

12. **BUY HIGH-QUALITY NUTRITIOUS FOOD.** Remember, eating an abundance of fresh fruits and vegetables, whole grains, and nuts will keep you healthy so you don't need to spend your food money on as many medications. Especially eat more fresh fruits and vegetables. Remember what your mother taught you as a child about eating plenty of fresh fruits and vegetables every day.

13. **INCLUDE A VARIETY OF COLOR.** If you eat antioxidant-rich foods in the form of colorful fruits and vegetables, you will cut down on the need for expensive synthetic vitamins. Remember this when planning menus to include foods of various colors, especially the deep greens and bright reds.

BENEFITS OF FRUITS AND VEGETABLES

Fruits and vegetables contain essential vitamins, minerals, and fiber that reduce the risk of a number of chronic diseases, including cardiovascular disease, stroke, and certain kinds of cancers. We can all benefit from these nutritious fruits and vegetables that are a natural source of energy. And the fruits and vegetables come in fabulous colors and flavors. Eat a variety of colorful fruits and vegetables every day to get healthy and stay healthy.

Ideas for Planning Well-Balanced Meals

There are many different options for a well-balanced plant-based diet. Let's take a look first at breakfast and see what is cooking.

APPLESAUCE on toast with fresh fruit   Oatmeal with soymilk, fresh fruit, raisin toast, nuts, and se

BREAKFAST: It is important to start the day off right with a hearty, nutritious breakfast.

OATMEAL PANCAKES, applesauce, and fresh fruit

Cedar Lake® Chops, Terkettes, and Pecan Patties

DINNER: When transitioning to a plant-based diet, it may be helpful to use some of the commercial vegetarian protein foods. Here are some good options.

Spaghetti, vegetarian meatballs, peas, and salad

Vegetarian **CHOPS**, **OVEN-BROWNED POTATOES**, carrots, and salad

Chops

Chops (Cedar Lake® brand)   Breading Meal (Cedar Lake® brand)

ROLL chops in breading meal. **SAUTÉ** in olive oil until brown. **TURN** and **BROWN** on the other side.

Be sure to include a fresh vegetable salad every day when you are planning your menu.

Salad

1 bag of mixed greens
2 tomatoes
1 cucumber
2 carrots
1 avocado
1 red onion

MIX and **SERVE**.

SUPPER: Following are photographs of simple suppers.

Mixed green **SALAD**

STRAWBERRY TOFU ALMOND SMOOTHIE
Recipe is on page 97 of the *Natural Lifestyle Cooking* workbook.

A simple supper option is fresh fruit, **ZWIEBACK**, **CRISPY OAT CAKES**, and cereal coffee.

MAKE ALL MEALS A PLEASANT EXPERIENCE. Simple suppers can be a fun time for the children. A game of Scrabble with some popcorn and smoothies for a Saturday-evening family night can be very beneficial for building family relationships. It is simple, easy, and fun.

PLANNING A BALANCED DIET: CONCLUSION

Based on what we put into our bodies, we determine how well our bodies will function. We can reduce the risk of many of the diseases that are plaguing people around the world in the twenty-first century. Our choices may determine whether we die prematurely from a heart attack, cancer, stroke, diabetes, obesity, and a host of other physical problems. To a certain

Popcorn, apples, and smoothies are great for a family night of fun and games.

extent we can control whether we get sick or stay well by making the right lifestyle choices. To achieve good health, it is important to live according to God's natural laws. Good health is necessary to enjoy life to the fullest. Here is some good news. We can experience better health by choosing to fix healthful meals and follow the eight principles of WELLNESS. (See pages 173–189 in the *Natural Lifestyle Cooking* cookbook for further information on WELLNESS.)

We cannot improve on the Creator's plan given in the beginning. The plant-based vegetarian diet given in the Bible's first book, Genesis, is still the diet that is the very best for our total health and well-being.

ANSWERS FOR CLASS 3

1. Chronic diseases are long-term diseases that are largely preventable, such as heart disease, cancer, diabetes, and osteoporosis.

2. Diet is one of the main factors in treating chronic diseases, and eating a plant-based diet can help reduce the risk of these diseases.

3. A. Fruits and vegetables; B. Milk; C. Meat; D. Cereals and breads.

4. MyPlate

5. Healthy Eating Plate

6. Foods high in antioxidants—fruit, vegetables, nuts and seeds, grains, and legumes.

7. Variety of color

8. A. Right kind. B. Right amount. C. Right times.

9. Three for most people; two for some people. (If you are a diabetic, consult your physician.)

ENDNOTES

1.   http://www.who.int/topics/chronic_diseases/en/.
2.   "History of USDA Nutrition Guides," *Wikipedia*, accessed April 23, 2013, http://en.wikipedia.org/wiki/History_ofUSDA _nutrition_guides.
3.   Accessed April 23, 2013, http://www.pcrm.org/health/diets/.
4.   "The Four Food Groups, Old and New," accessed April 23, 2013, http://www.jewishveg.com/schwartz/ffgroups.html.
5.   Ibid.
6.   "Harvard Researchers Unveil New Healthy Eating Plate," ABC News, accessed April 24, 2013, http://abcnews.go.com /Health/harvard-researchers-offer-alternative-usdas-myplate/story?id=14519983.
7.   Ibid.
8.   "Harvard to USDA: Check Out the Healthy Eating Plate," *Harvard Health Blog,* accessed April 23, 2013, http://www.health .harvard.edu/blog/harvard-to-usda-check-out-the-healthy-eating-plate-201109143344.
9.   Ibid.
10.   "Healthy Eating Plate," The Nutrition Source, accessed May 21, 2013, http://www.hsph.harvard.edu/nutritionsource/healthy -eating-plate.
11.   White, *Counsels on Diet and Foods,* 310.
12.   "Antioxidants and Cancer Prevention: Fact Sheet," Cancer, accessed April 23, 2013, http://www.cancer.gov/cancertopics /factsheet/prevent.
13.   "20 Common Foods With the Most Antioxidants," Web MD, accessed April 24, 2013, http://www.webmd.com/food -recipes/20-common-foods-most-antioxidants.
14.   White, *Counsels on Diet and Foods,* 173, 174.
15.   Ibid., 176.
16.   Ibid., 178.
17.   Neil Nedley, *Proof Positive,* 43.
18.   White, *Counsels on Diet and Foods,* 176.

Class 4

Advantages of a Total Vegetarian Diet

Entrées · Protein

The **scientific evidence** is in, and it's conclusive. A **balanced total vegetarian diet is better** for you than one that includes meat. A host of comparative studies have demonstrated this fact. For example, males who regularly eat meat have been found to suffer from twice as many fatal coronary heart attacks than vegetarian males.[1] And this is just the beginning of the story.

In a *New England Journal of Medicine* article, the authors report a study of 80,082 women from thirty-four to fifty-nine years old with no known coronary artery disease or stroke. The health habits and lifestyle of these women were followed for fourteen years. The study concluded that "each increase of 5% energy intake from saturated fat as compared to an equivalent intake from carbohydrates was associated with a 17% risk of coronary heart disease."[2] In other words, **reduce your saturated fats from animal products and increase your consumption of fruits, vegetables, nuts, and legumes,** and you will **reduce the possibility of a heart attack.**

1. WHAT ARE THE TOP MAJOR CAUSES OF DEATH IN THE UNITED STATES?

LEADING CAUSES OF DEATH IN THE UNITED STATES[3]

- Heart disease: 597,689
- Cancer: 574,743
- Chronic lower respiratory diseases: 138,080

- Stroke (cerebrovascular diseases): 129,476
- Accidents (unintentional injuries): 120,859
- Alzheimer's disease: 83,494
- Diabetes: 69,071

Multiple scientific studies reveal that we can reduce the risk of heart disease by reducing the fat content in our recipes and eating a plant-based diet.

2. HOW CAN THESE DISEASES BE PREVENTED?

Medical researchers have discovered that **some foods are protective** against the killer diseases of the twenty-first century. These **protective foods are plant-based foods such as fruits, nuts, grains, and vegetables.** Population groups who eat a wide variety of **plant-based foods have reduced their risk of both heart disease and cancer.** So it is obvious that diet plays a significant role in lowering our risk of degenerative diseases, which are the leading killers in the twenty-first century.

WHY BE A TOTAL VEGETARIAN?

A growing number of Americans are either limiting the amount of meat they eat or are eliminating it altogether. According to a recent survey, some 7.3 million Americans claim they are vegetarians, while 22.8 million follow a "vegetarian-inclined" diet.[4] Vegetarianism is steadily growing in popularity. This lesson discusses several **reasons for you to seriously consider choosing a plant-based diet.**

DECREASE YOUR RISK OF A HEART ATTACK

3. HOW MANY DEATHS IN THE UNITED STATES EACH YEAR ARE DUE TO CORONARY ARTERY DISEASE?

There are **many advantages in adopting a total vegetarian diet.** From a health standpoint, it is certainly an advantage to markedly **reduce** your meat intake and gradually **cut it out** altogether. According to the Centers for Disease Control and Prevention Web site, every year there are over 600,000 deaths in the United States due to **coronary artery disease and stroke.** Heart disease is the leading cause of death for both men and women.[5] One important key in reducing heart-attack deaths is **reducing animal fat** in the diet. "Since 1960 rates for chronic diseases have changed dramatically. Heart disease rates have dropped by almost two thirds in the last fifty years."[6] Multiple well-known scientific studies reveal that we can overwhelmingly reduce our potential for heart disease by reducing the fat content and eating a plant-based diet.

In Japan, Greece, and Italy, where levels of blood cholesterol are low compared to the average American levels, the rate of heart attacks is lower than in the United States. According to the *Journal of American Medicine,* every time we reduce our cholesterol level by 1 percent, we reduce our risk of heart disease by 2 percent. In other words, if you reduce your total cholesterol from 300 mg/dl to 200 mg/dl (a one-third reduction), you reduce your risk of a heart attack by two-thirds.[7]

WHAT IS CHOLESTEROL?

Cholesterol is a **fatty substance** manufactured by the body and is **present in all foods of animal origin. Vegetable products do not contain cholesterol.** Some plant foods contain limited amounts of fat, which the body may use to produce cholesterol, but only animal products contain cholesterol that can be ingested directly. Most cholesterol enters the blood and is transported around in packets called lipoproteins. These microscopic particles are made up largely of fat, cholesterol, and protein. They act like trucks, carrying cholesterol away from the local scene. A problem occurs when excess cholesterol is not carried away. It is then deposited on the arterial walls, leading to hardening of the arteries and potentially **resulting in coronary artery disease.**

HOW TO EVALUATE YOUR PERSONAL RISK OF A HEART ATTACK

A heart attack generally is not caused by one single factor. Most often it is the result of multiple factors. Medical researchers list **ten risk factors contributing to heart attacks.**[8] As we review these major risk factors, place a check mark in the box beside any risk factor that applies to you.

RISK FACTOR	PLACE CHECK MARK HERE
1. Male	❑
2. Hereditary factors	❑
3. Little physical activity	❑
4. Inner stress	❑
5. Elevated blood cholesterol (over 200 mg)	❑
6. High blood pressure	❑
7. Overweight (more than 10 lbs.)	❑
8. Cigarette smoker	❑
9. Diabetes/Pre-diabetes	❑
10. Insufficient sleep (consistently less than six hours per night)	❑

As few as **two risk factors** indicate the **need of dietary control. Three or four risk factors** indicate **the probability of heart disease,** while over **five necessitates immediate attention.** It is interesting to note that at least **four** of the ten are related to **diet.** It is also possible to do something about eight of the above ten risk factors. We can make choices to change faulty lifestyle habit patterns into positive, health-building ones.

DIETARY CONTROL OF CHOLESTEROL

Because dietary fat (amount and type) is directly related to coronary heart disease, a **blood cholesterol of over 250 mg** presents four times the risk of a heart attack than one under 200 mg.

THE FOLLOWING PRACTICAL STEPS WILL HELP LOWER HARMFUL FORMS OF CHOLESTEROL:

- **CHANGE** the type of fat in your diet from animal to vegetable.
- **USE** nut milk or soymilk in place of cow's milk.
- **ELIMINATE** the use of meat products.
- **LIMIT** the use of fried foods.
- **CONTROL** the intake of sugars in all forms (white, brown, raw, etc.).
- **EAT** a wide variety of whole grains, fruits, nuts and seeds, and vegetables.

Make these few changes and you will reduce your risk of heart disease.

DECREASE YOUR RISK OF CANCER

Research demonstrates the value of a plant-based diet in reducing the risk of cancer, another leading cause of death. The results of these studies lead us back to God's original diet in the Garden of Eden at Creation.

"There is overwhelming evidence that cancer is related to the environment and diet is a large factor, perhaps the major environmental factor."[9]

British epidemiologist Richard Doll believes food is number one in accounting for 35 percent of all tumors.[10] "Dr. Gio B. Gori, former deputy director of the National Cancer Institute, believes that 30 percent of cancer in women and 40 percent of cancer in men are the result of a poor diet that is high in both sugar and fat."[11]

In the newly released findings of the Adventist Health Study-2, funded by the National Institutes of Health, researchers reported that "vegan [plant-based] diets showed statistically significant protection for overall cancer incidence . . . in both genders combined and for female specific cancers. . . . Lacto-ovo vegetarians appeared to be associated with decreased risk of cancers of the gastro-intestinal system."[12]

4. WHAT ARE SOME STEPS WE CAN TAKE TO GREATLY REDUCE THE RISK OF CANCER? ELIMINATE OR GREATLY REDUCE:

A. _____

B. _____

C. _____

D. _____

Eliminating tobacco is the primary way of reducing the risk of lung cancer. The American Institute for Cancer Research lists the following three ways of reducing the risk of all cancers.

- **WEIGHT**—Aim to be a healthy weight throughout life.
- **DIET**—Choose plant foods, reduce red meat, and eliminate all processed food.
  - ✓ Reduce or eliminate animal products.
  - ✓ Reduce visible fats.
  - ✓ Reduce excessive sugar.
  - ✓ Reduce refined foods.
- **PHYSICAL ACTIVITY**—Be physically active every day in any way for at least thirty minutes and be sure to get adequate sunshine and vitamin D.

5. WHAT DOES A CANCER-PREVENTION DIET INCLUDE?

One hundred years ago, the major killers were pneumonia, influenza, tuberculosis, infection, and infant mortality. Modern medicine has greatly reduced and largely eliminated these killers. Today's killers are brought about largely by faulty lifestyle choices we can do something about. **We can choose to take control of our lives and health.** No matter what condition we find ourselves in, it is never too late to make positive choices.

DECREASE RISK OF ANIMAL-TO-HUMAN COMMUNICABLE DISEASES

There is a continuing, increasing risk of animal diseases transmitting to humans. **Salmonellosis, brucellosis, and trichinosis may be transmitted.** *Trichinosis* is generally transmitted through infected, poorly cooked pork products. *Brucellosis* is highly contagious and is caused by the ingestion of unsterilized milk or meat from infected animals. Its symptoms are fevers, muscular pain, and sweating lasting from a few weeks to many months. *Salmonellosis* is an infection often contracted from incorrectly prepared poultry, pork, and beef. It can also be contracted from eggs and dairy products that are not prepared, handled, or refrigerated properly.

Of more than **two hundred communicable diseases of animals, one hundred are considered infectious to man,** and **eighty are transmitted** naturally between vertebrate animals and man. "Every year there are 40,000 cases of salmonellosis reported in the United States but the number may actually be 30 times or more greater. Beef, poultry, milk and eggs are the foods most often infected with salmonellosis."[13]

DECREASE YOUR RISK OF CONSUMING CONCENTRATED PESTICIDES

In addition to transmission of diseases, meats can also sicken through pesticide contamination. Lewis Regenstein, in his book *How to Survive in America the Poisoned,* writes, "Meat contains approximately 14 times more pesticides than do plant foods. . . . Thus, by eating foods of animal origin, one ingests greatly concentrated amounts of hazardous chemicals."[14]

Meats have far higher concentrates of pesticides than fruits and vegetables. Interestingly enough, the highest concentrate of pesticide is in nonorganic butter. Because toxins tend to concentrate in fatty tissues, you can reduce your exposure to potentially harmful chemicals by reducing or eliminating the meat and increasing the fruits and vegetables in your diet.

INCREASE YOUR ENDURANCE

The ideal diet should not only reduce the risk of disease but give us the greatest "go power" possible. Per-Olof Astrand, MD, conducted a study of Swedish men to determine the best diet for athletes. In the study, athletes were given a bicycle endurance test to discover their maximum exercise time.

BICYCLE ENDURANCE TEST[15]

Diet	Exercise Time
Meat and protein diet	60 minutes
Mixed fuel diet (protein and carbohydrate)	120 minutes
Vegetarian diet	180 minutes

The group on the vegetarian diet performed nearly three times longer than those on the meat diet.

For decades some of the world's super athletes have been or are vegetarians. Here are a few examples.[16]

- **BILL PEARL**—four-time Mr. Universe.

- **LIZZIE ARNETSTEAD**—2012 Olympic silver medal winner in the grueling eighty-seven-mile cycle race.

- **EDWIN MOSES**—Olympic gold medalist in 440-meter hurdles. He won 122 successive races between 1977 and 1987.

- **BODE MILLER**—One of the greatest American skiers of all time. Winner of five Olympic medals.

- **CARL LEWIS**—Eventually became a vegan vegetarian and won a gold medal at the age of thirty in 1991 in the one hundred-meter race and set a world record.

- **TONY GONZALEZ**—National Football League, Hall of Fame tight end.

- **MIKE TYSON**—Professional boxer.

- **JOE NAMATH**—Professional football player.

These are just a few of the world-famous athletes in all sports who are vegetarians.

IMPROVE USE OF LAND AND RESOURCES

"An acre of land planted in soybeans can produce ten times as much protein as animals grazing on the same land. A pound of beef costs four times as much to produce as a pound of non-meat protein. According to one estimate, food raised on one acre of land and converted into beef will fill the protein needs of a single person for 77 days. But soybeans raised on the same acre can fill his needs for 6.1 years."[17]

PROVIDE ADEQUATE PROTEIN

6. CAN A PLANT-BASED DIET PROVIDE ADEQUATE NUTRITION, INCLUDING PROTEIN? (SEE *NATURAL LIFESTYLE COOKING* COOKBOOK, PAGES 62, 63.)

According to the National Academy of Sciences, National Research Council, which publishes the Recommended Daily Allowances for U.S. food, "All but the most restricted vegetarian diets are nutritionally safe. The most important safeguard for the average vegetarian consumer is great variety in the diet."[18]

As long as total vegetarians eat a wide variety of fruits, nuts, grains, and vegetables, they will get all the nutrients necessary for good nutrition—with one possible exception, vitamin B_{12}.

Although many vegetarians never have problems with a vitamin B_{12} deficiency, others do.

For this reason, most nutrition experts recommend all total vegetarians take a daily vitamin B$_{12}$ supplement as a safeguard.[19]

7. WHY DO WE NEED PROTEINS? (FOR MORE INFORMATION ON PROTEIN, SEE *NATURAL LIFESTYLE COOKING* COOKBOOK, PAGES 63, 64.)

Proteins are composed of chains of amino acids. Amino acids that cannot be made by the body are called essential amino acids. These **essential amino acids** must be present in our food. **Plant protein is not lacking in essential amino acids.** When we eat plant foods, the plant proteins are reassembled by our digestive systems into the various amino acids. These amino acids are absorbed into the blood stream and then utilized by our bodies to construct all the proteins we need to build and repair body tissues. Recent studies have found that there are **significant benefits** from **consuming plant proteins.** Although **a single plant may not provide all the essential amino acids, plant proteins eaten in combination do.**

8. WHAT ARE THE SIGNIFICANT BENEFITS OF CONSUMING PLANT PROTEIN VERSUS ANIMAL PROTEIN?

A. _____

B. _____

C. _____

D. _____

E. _____

F. _____

G. _____

Plant proteins **lower blood cholesterol, reduce the risk of certain cancers,** and contribute to **lowering our blood pressure.** They also **improve the symptoms of type 2 diabetes** as well as **enhancing vigor and endurance.** Overall, plant protein **contributes to a longer life.**

9. WHAT IS THE DAILY RECOMMENDED AMOUNT OF PROTEIN?

MEN _____

WOMEN _____

CHILDREN _____

The recommended daily amount of protein for **women** is approximately **46 grams. Men** require about **56 grams. Children** require between **13 and 34 grams** of protein daily, the requirement varies with age and body weight. If we **eat a wide variety of fruits, nuts, grains, vegetables, and legumes** with adequate calories, we will certainly get **sufficient amounts of protein.**

10. WHAT PLANT FOODS ARE GOOD SOURCES OF PROTEIN? (SEE *NATURAL LIFESTYLE COOKING* COOKBOOK, PAGE 64.)

A. _____

B. _____

C. _____

PROTEIN RECIPES

Quinoa Patties

2 c. cooked quinoa
1 c. walnuts, chopped fine
½ c. ground raw cashews
¼ c. ground flaxseed
1 c. whole-wheat bread crumbs
1 T. olive oil
1 onion, chopped
3 cloves garlic, minced
¼ c. chopped celery

½ c. water
½ t. salt
1 T. McKays® chicken-style seasoning
1 T. Bragg® Liquid Aminos
2 T. nutritional yeast
1 t. Italian seasoning
1 t. egg replacer mixed with 2 T. water
1 T. gluten flour

MIX all ingredients. **FORM** into patties. **SAUTÉ** in olive oil until golden brown. **TURN** and brown on the other side.

Boston Baked Beans

1 lb. navy or Great Northern beans boiled in
   approximately 10 c. water
2 ½ c. water
1 whole onion
½ c. molasses
¼ c. brown sugar
¾ t. salt
2 T. Earth Balance® margarine spread

WASH and **SORT** beans. **PLACE** in large
kettle. **ADD** 10 cups water and **BRING** to a boil.
BOIL 5 minutes. **REMOVE** from heat. **LET
STAND** covered for 60 minutes. **BRING** to a
boil and **BOIL** for 60 minutes. **DRAIN** water
and **ADD** the additional 2 ½ cups water and
all other ingredients. **BAKE** at 275°F for 5 to 6
hours. Note: Add more liquid if needed.

Millet Patties

3 c. cooked millet
1 c. raw cashews
1 ½ c. water
1 onion, chopped
2 cloves garlic,
   minced
1 c. quick oats
1 c. firm tofu, mashed

1 ½ c. bread crumbs
2 T. ground flaxseeds
2 T. Bragg® Liquid
   Aminos
½ t. oregano
½ t. sage
1 t. salt

BLEND cashews and water. **MIX** all
ingredients together. **FORM** into patties.
SAUTÉ in oiled skillet until brown. **TURN**
and **SAUTÉ** on the other side. Note: If you
choose, you can bake the burgers instead of
cooking them in a skillet.

COMMON-SENSE STEPS TO BECOMING A TOTAL VEGETARIAN

Develop a plan to eat a plant-based total vegetarian diet. Decide to put this definite plan into practice. Commit yourself to living a positive, healthy lifestyle, and watch the benefits that you will receive as you put these principles into practice in your life. The steps below will help you in your journey to eating a total plant-based diet.

- **Begin by increasing** your intake of **fruits and vegetables.**
- **Experiment** with a wide selection of **vegetarian protein dishes** until you discover the ones your family really enjoys.
- **Substitute** these tasty, nutritious **vegetarian dishes** at least twice a week for your regular **meat dishes.** During a transition period, meat analogues from companies such as Cedar Lake Foods, Loma Linda Foods, Worthington Foods, Morning Star Farms, and others may be helpful.
- **Cut out** all meat high in saturated fats, such as **pork, marbled steaks, hamburgers, hot dogs,** etc.
- **Cut empty calories** (sugars and visible fats) at least in half.
- Because lifestyle change is best achieved gradually, give yourself a period of three to six months to make the **complete transition.**
- Your taste buds will begin to adapt as you **develop a new taste** for wholesome foods such as nut roasts, peas, beans, lentils, whole grains, and gluten meat substitutes.

A **total vegetarian** diet will go a long way to bring your family health and longevity. The vegetarian diet is not new. It dates back to the Garden of Eden. It was **God's original diet** for the human race. After all, when the Creator made this world, He gave us an abundance of fruits, nuts, grains, and vegetables in the Garden of Eden. This world needs a little more of the Eden life—a life of health, harmony, and happiness; a life of inner peace, physical well-being, and a closeness with our Creator. In the hectic pace of twenty-first-century living, the diet from nature's pantry will strengthen both our minds and bodies. The One who made us and loves us with an everlasting love longs for us to be healthy. He provided **nature's diet** at the beginning **to give us optimum health.**

My wish for you is that you eat well, be well, stay well, prosper, and be in health.

ANSWERS FOR CLASS 4

1. Heart disease, cancer, stroke
2. By changing our dietary habits
3. 600,000 deaths
4. A. Animal products

   B. Visible fats
   C. Excessive sugar
   D. Highly refined foods

5. Fruits, nuts and seeds, grains, and vegetables

6. Yes, by eating a wide variety of fruits, nuts and seeds, grains, and vegetables.

7. To build and repair body tissues

8. A. Lowers blood cholesterol
   B. Lowers high blood pressure
   C. Lowers risk of certain cancers
   D. Lowers risk of osteoporosis
   E. Improves diabetes symptoms
   F. Enhances vigor and endurance
   G. Lengthens life span

9. Men—56 grams
   Women—46 grams
   Children—13 to 34 grams varying with age and body weight

10. A. Whole grains
    B. Legumes
    C. Nuts

ENDNOTES

1.   Michael F. Jacobson, *Six Arguments for a Greener Diet,* 23, accessed March 19, 2013, http://www.cspinet.org/EatingGreen.
2.   F. B. Hu, et al., "Dietary Fat Intake and Coronary Heart Disease in Women," *New England Journal of Medicine* 337, no. 21 (November 20, 1997): 1491–1499.
3.   "Deaths and Mortality," Centers for Disease Control and Prevention, http://www.cdc.gov/nchs/fastats/death.htm.
4.   "Vegetarianism in America," accessed March 19, 2013, http://www.vegetariantimes.com/article/vegetarianism-in-America.
5.   "Heart Disease Facts," accessed March 19, 2013, http://www.cdc.gov/heartdisease/facts.htm.
6.   Patrick Remington and Ross C. Brownson, "Fifty Years of Progress in Chronic Disease and Epidemiology and Control," Centers for Disease Control and Prevention, *Morbidity and Mortality Weekly Report* 60, no. 4 (October 7, 2011): 70–77.
7.   Lipid Research Clinics Program, "The Lipid Research Coronary Primary Prevention Trial Results II" 251, no. 3 (1984): 365–374.
8.   "Coronary Artery Disease—Coronary Heart Disease," accessed March 19, 2013, http://www.heart.org/HEARTORG/Conditions/More/MyHeartandStrokeNews/Coronary-Artery-Disease---coronary-heart-disease_UCM_436416_article.jsp.
9.   D. M. Hegsted, *Chicago Tribune,* August 10, 1983.
10. Richard Doll and Richard Peto, "The Causes of Cancer: Quantitative Estimates of Avoidable Risks of Cancer in the United States Today," *Journal of the National Cancer Institute* 66, no. 6 (1981).
11. Gio B. Gori and Brian J. Richter, "Macro Economics of Disease Prevention in the United States," *Science Magazine* 200 (June 9, 1978): 1124–1130.
12. Y. Tantananego-Bartley, K. Jaceldo-Siegl, J. Fan, G. Fraser, "Vegetarian Diets and the Incidence of Cancer in a Low Risk Population," *Cancer Epidemiology Biomarkers & Prevention* (February 22, 2013): 286–294.
13. "Salmonellosis," Centers for Disease Control and Prevention, http://www.cdc.gov/nczved/divisions/dfbmd/diseases/salmonellosis/#what.
14. Lewis Regenstein, *How to Survive America the Poisoned,* quoted in Frank Addleman, *The Winning Edge: Nutrition for Athletic Fitness and Performance* (New York: Prentice Hall, 1987), 64.
15. Addleman, *The Winning Edge,* 64.
16. www.peta.org/b/thepetafiles/archive/2011/05/24/peta-s-top-10-vegetarian-athletes.aspx; see also www.veganathlete.com/vegan-vegetarian atheletes.php.
17. National Soybean Research Laboratory, accessed March 25, 2013, http://www.nsrl.uiuc.edu/soy_benefits.html.
18. Donald W. Oliver and Kathleen Waldron Gershman, *Education, Modernity, and Fractured Meaning* (Albany, N.Y.: State University of New York, 1989), 222; see also Florence G. Korchin, *Science in the Marketplace* (Culver City, Calif.: Tiger Publications, 1995), 28.
19. Reed Mangels, "Vitamin B12 in the Vegan Diet," accessed March 27, 2013, http://www.vrg.org/nutrition/b12.php.

Class 5

Simple, Healthful Suppers

Suppers · Family Meals · Immune System · Weight Control

I n this lesson we will discuss the **value of simple suppers in maintaining health and in combating obesity.** We will also analyze the best foods to include in those light evening meals.

Surveys conducted for the Gallup-Healthways Well-Being Index reported that **62.8 percent of all Americans are obese or overweight!** Changing your meal schedule by eating simple, healthful suppers is a wise choice if you are interested in shedding some of those extra pounds.[1] A sensible approach to reducing weight is eating a **well-balanced nutritious diet, exercising regularly,** and **eating the right amounts** at the **right times.** A light evening meal will certainly help you achieve your optimal weight.

Supper is the term used to describe a **less formal, simpler light family evening meal.** This meal has been traditionally eaten after a main meal in the middle of the day. Although the expression supper is often used interchangeably with the term *dinner,* they are actually two different kinds of meals. Traditionally, dinner has been the main and most formal meal of the day.

Until the eighteenth century, dinner was eaten as the midday meal. Supper was ordinarily the last meal of the day. The normal order was **breakfast-dinner-supper.** When lifestyles changed and the evening meal became the main meal of the day, the name *dinner* followed it, and the noon meal was called lunch. When it comes to weight control, it might be better to get back to eating dinner, the main meal, in the middle of the day whenever possible and the light meal in the evening. Then the order would again be **BREAKFAST— DINNER—SUPPER instead of** BREAKFAST—LUNCH—DINNER.

Because our **schedules vary,** it is necessary to **adapt the principles of health** in the context of our family needs. It does take effort to prepare and time meals to best accommodate our family's schedules. If you have young **children who are in school,** it may be more difficult to eat your main meal in the middle of the day. In this case, it is important to plan on eating as early as possible in the evening. Do the best you can to **provide the most nutritious meals** for your family **at the most appropriate times.**

When our three children were in school, it was challenging to eat a main meal in the middle of the day. During their school years, we planned to eat as early in the evening as possible. **Dinner** in the evening became our main meal of the day. We ate regularly at about 5:30 P.M. Our **breakfast** was at about 7:30 A.M. and **lunch** at 12:30 P.M. This seemed to work very well for us. Now at this stage of life, my husband and I have a little more flexible schedule, so we plan to eat a hearty, nutritious, and substantial **breakfast** at around 8:00 to 8:15 A.M., and a well-balanced **dinner** around 1:00 to 1:15 P.M. If we eat **supper** at all, it is extremely light with fruit and toast or simple soup at approximately 6:00 to 6:15 P.M.

We recognize that in the busy, hectic world we live in, it is **often difficult to set the ideal time for eating.** Our work necessitates a lot of travel. Often we have to eat away from home, and often we eat with others. In order to **socialize with family and friends** during meals, we have attempted to plan our meals at times that are common to most people. Considering work, travel, and the desire to socialize, having a regular set time to eat can be challenging.

FAMILY MEALS

Family mealtimes provide quality family time. Recent research reveals the **importance of establishing regular mealtimes with the family.** A study directed by Gary L. Hopkins, MD, DrPH, a research professor at Andrews University, found that family meals made a difference in the lives of most young people. A program called **Project EAT** explored the association between the frequency of family meals and the psychosocial well-being of adolescent boys and girls.

The data analysis from this research showed that the **frequency of family meals was associated with numerous benefits:**

- **BETTER HEALTHY EATING HABITS.** Family meals have the potential of impacting the diets of children. "One study conducted on adolescents indicated that those who watched television during meals were found to have lower intakes of vegetables, calcium-rich food, and grains. They also had higher intakes of soft drinks compared to adolescents not watching television during meals."[2]

- **BETTER DIETARY QUALITY AND MEAL PATTERNS.** Dietary quality is critical for good health. It is extremely important for children to establish good habits early in life. The study concluded that family meals during adolescence may have a lasting positive influence on dietary quality and meal patterns in young adulthood.

- **BETTER WEIGHT CONTROL.** With obesity on the rise, eating together may be one of the answers to reducing childhood obesity. Family meals have the potential to substantially impact the dietary intake of children. In research among kids attending alternative schools, students who reported never eating family meals were more likely to be overweight and to eat less fruit. They also ate fewer breakfasts and tended to be more depressed.[3]

- **BETTER ACADEMIC PERFORMANCE.** Studies showed that if children ate with their families, they were more likely to have higher grades in school and to attend college. The Hopkins study also stated, "In an analysis of research that we [Hopkins and McBride] are conducting at the present time, high school students who are present for at least three family meals per week are nearly twice as likely to get A's in school."[4]

- **BETTER OPPORTUNITIES FOR SOCIALIZATION WITH FAMILY.** Whatever meal you can share with the family can be the most important meal of the day. A study done by the Kraft company found that American families who eat together are happier in many aspects of their lives than those who don't. Children and teens who eat family meals together experience improved family communication, have stronger family ties, and a greater sense of identity and belonging. A study of family eating patterns published by the National Center on Addiction and Substance Abuse (CASA) at Columbia University found that **children in families who do not regularly eat together are more than twice as likely than those who have frequent meals together to say there is a great deal of tension among family members.** They are also much less likely to think their parents are proud of them. **Communication during meals gives the family an opportunity to bond.**[5]

- **LESS SUBSTANCE ABUSE.** A follow-up study on the first family dinner study (sponsored by the National Center on Addiction and Substance Abuse) reported that the frequency of family meals was associated with less substance abuse. The research has consistently shown that teenagers who eat dinner more often with their families are less likely to use alcohol, smoke cigarettes, or use other harmful, illicit drugs.[6]

- **LESS THEFT** and reduced interest in gang membership. One study "reported the frequency of family meals also was associated with less theft and reduced interest in gang membership."[7]

- **LESS DISORDERED EATING BEHAVIORS.** Studies from Project EAT have found that adolescents, particularly girls, who report more frequent family meals are less likely to engage in disordered eating behaviors than adolescents eating fewer family meals.

- **LESS HIGH-RISK BEHAVIORS AMONG ADOLESCENTS.** "More than half of teens who don't eat dinner with their parents have sexual relations by age 15 or 16. This rate decreases to 32 percent when there are family meals in the home. Teens who have meals with their families are also less likely to have suicidal thoughts or suicidal attempts, and are less likely to ever be suspended from school."[8]

- **BETTER FAITH.** "Research by the Search Institute confirms that the most significant religious influence on children is not what happens at church, but what happens at home."[9] Eating family meals together is a very important time when beliefs and values are developed and core values established.

1. **LIST SOME OF THE PHYSICAL, MENTAL, SOCIAL, BEHAVIORAL, AND SPIRITUAL BENEFITS OF FAMILY MEALS.**

   A. PHYSICAL _____

B. MENTAL _____

C. SOCIAL _____

D. BEHAVIORAL _____

E. SPIRITUAL _____

You have probably heard the old saying, "A family who prays together, stays together." We might coin new mottoes: **"At the family table, kids become stable,"** or **"Eating together helps our kids keep it together."** Families who eat together have children who are more physically healthy, mentally alert, socially adjusted, better behaved, and spiritually committed. The psalmist describes the blessings that come to a godly home gathered around the family table. "Your wife shall be like a fruitful vine in the very heart of your house, your children like olive plants all around your table. Behold, thus shall the man be blessed who fears the LORD" (Psalm 128:3, 4).

TIPS FOR MAKING FAMILY MEALTIMES ENJOYABLE

- **PLACE PRIORITY** on family meals.
- **ESTABLISH REGULAR** mealtimes.
- **PLAN** to **EAT** at least **ONE MEAL** a day **TOGETHER** with the entire family.
- **MAKE MEALTIMES SPECIAL.**
- **PREPARE** wholesome, **DELICIOUS** food.
- **INVOLVE** the family. Let them help make the food, set the table, and clean up.
- **TAKE PLENTY OF TIME.** Don't rush. Plan to spend forty-five minutes to an hour eating together at least once a day.
- **FOCUS ON THE FAMILY. TURN OFF** all electronic communication devices—TV, cell phones, iPads, etc.
- Create a **RELAXING ENVIRONMENT.**
- **TALK** to your children. Have pleasant discussions with them.
- **CREATE A POSITIVE ATMOSPHERE.** Avoid controversial discussions.
- **LAUGH A LOT.** "A merry heart does good, like medicine" (Proverbs 17:22). Make it a pleasant time for the entire family.
- **LOOK FORWARD** to family mealtime as the **BEST PART OF THE DAY.**

OBESITY EPIDEMIC

Obesity is a very serious problem, and unless we change our lifestyles, our eating habits, and the amount of physical activity we get each day, the trend will only become worse. Weight control needs to be a global priority.

The World Health Organization predicts there will be **2.3 billion overweight adults in the world by 2015** and more than **700 million of them will be obese.**[10] The increase of fast, convenient foods, labor-saving devices, sedentary jobs, and motorized transportation is a sure means of people getting heavier.

2. **WHAT PERCENTAGE OF AMERICANS ARE OBESE OR OVERWEIGHT?**

    A. **OBESE** _____

    B. **OVERWEIGHT** _____

    C. **TOTAL** _____

According to the **most recent statistics** from the Centers for Disease Control and Prevention, a whopping **seventy-eight million adults—more than a third of the U.S. population—are obese.**[11] Eric Braverman, MD, founder of the New York neurology practice PATH Medical and a clinical assistant professor of integrative medicine at Weill Cornell Medical School, says that a more accurate number **could be up to twice that amount.**

Studies predict that 75 percent of people living in the United States will be overweight by 2015.[12] If people keep gaining weight at the current rate, being fat will be the norm, with 41 percent obese and 34 percent overweight.

WHAT CAUSES OBESITY?

3. **LIST TWO MAJOR REASONS FOR THE RECENT INCREASE OF OBESITY.**

    A. _____

    B. _____

POOR DIETARY HABITS—A lifestyle of poor dietary habits, such as eating a high-calorie diet, skipping breakfast, eating late at night, eating mostly fast food, and, of course, consuming high-empty-calorie beverages, contributes to the problem of obesity.

EATING TOO MANY CALORIES—The prime reason for obesity is simply **eating too much**—eating more calories than a person burns.

TOO LITTLE PHYSICAL ACTIVITY—One of the most serious, yet **correctible reasons for obesity is inactivity.** A lack of physical activity is a major cause of obesity. The more active we are, the more calories we will burn, and the more weight we will likely lose.

In addition to poor dietary habits, eating too many calories, and inactivity, there may be other factors that also play a role in obesity:

ENVIRONMENTAL FACTORS—A person's environment plays a significant role in obesity. Environmental factors **include lifestyle habits and behaviors.** Childhood obesity is on the rise in America. If the environment in the home is not conducive to children's health, it will be very difficult for them to control their weight. This is very true if there are not regular healthy meals. Snacking between meals adds to the problem. When inactivity is the norm due to the overuse of television or the Internet, it is difficult to control their weight. When the environment lends itself to inactivity because of family sedentary habits, obesity is inevitable. Take it upon yourself to encourage your family to exercise.

GENETICS—Genetics are an important factor in our health and understanding the problem of obesity. Obesity or thinness does tend to run in the family. But there is hope on the horizon. Lifestyle practices make a big difference. If you eat the right foods, in moderate quantities, at the right times, and maintain a regular exercise program, you can reduce your weight. Harvard School of Health posted this statement:

> "Genes influence every aspect of human physiology, development, and adaptation. Obesity is no exception." "What's increasingly clear from these early findings is that genetic factors identified so far make only a small contribution to obesity risk—and that our genes are not our destiny: Many people who carry these so-called 'obesity genes' do not become overweight, and healthy lifestyles can counteract these genetic effects. This article briefly outlines the contributions of genes and gene-environment interactions to the development of obesity."[13]

- **GENDER. Women** generally tend to be **more overweight** than men. Men have a higher resting metabolic rate (meaning they burn more energy when resting) than women, so men require more calories to maintain their body weight. When women become postmenopausal, their metabolic rate also decreases. This is one reason why many women gain weight after menopause.

- **AGE.** As we **get older,** our **body's ability to metabolize our food slows down.** As a result we do not require as many calories to maintain our ideal weight. Many people eat the same amount, but as they get older they gain weight. We **can't stop the aging process, so as we** approach the senior citizen years, we need to watch the calories and keep up the exercise routine.

In addition to overeating, inactivity, and environmental and genetic factors, there are a few more reasons why some people gain weight.

MEDICAL FACTORS—Although some people may have medical factors, these are not the prime cause of obesity. Medical factors may include hormone problems such as **hypothyroidism** (underactive thyroid that slows metabolism). This is a condition in which the thyroid gland produces too little thyroid hormone, slowing the metabolism and often causing weight gain. Some medical problems, such as **arthritis,** can lead to decreased activity, which may result in weight gain. For most people this is not the case. It is a matter of choosing to get obesity under control.

PSYCHOLOGICAL FACTORS—Psychological factors can also **influence our eating habits.** Some people eat in response to various negative emotions, such as stress, nervousness, disappointment, anger, or sadness. Other people suffer with **depression.** People who eat in response to these emotions usually eat junk foods, which are often high in calories and low in nutrients. They tend to overeat, causing obesity.

OVERCOMING OBESITY

Many overweight and obese people have **sedentary lifestyles.** They simply take in more calories than they burn through exercise. If we consume most of the calories in the evening, sleep less, skip breakfast, and eat in between meals, we will likely gain weight. Weight control requires a balance between the calories we consume and the calories we expend. A simple principle is that **when calorie intake exceeds calorie expenditure,** we will gain weight. The cure sounds simple: just eat less and exercise more. Unfortunately, it is more complicated than that because weight gain often occurs gradually over many years. The reversal also **involves an entire lifestyle change,** including a healthy diet, increased exercise, and discipline in both the quantity and times we eat. Of course there are some people who struggle with hereditary and genetic issues, but even they need not give up in despair. **The principles in this lesson will be extremely helpful.**

4. **LIST THREE GOOD WAYS FOR US TO CONTROL OUR WEIGHT.**

    A. _____

    B. _____

    C. _____

It is best for our health to **eat the lightest meal in the evening** so our stomach can rest with the rest of our body during our hours of sleep. If the stomach is full of undigested food, it will be difficult to get good, sound sleep. One of the **main reasons most people are not hungry at breakfast** time is that **they have eaten a large meal late in the evening.**

As early as the 1800s, health educators saw the effect of eating late at night. Ellen White, one of those early pioneers in health education, wrote:

"When we lie down at night, the stomach should have its work all done, that it, as well as other portions of the body, may enjoy rest. But if more food is forced upon it, the digestive organs are put in motion again, to perform the same round of labor through the sleeping hours. The sleep of such is often disturbed with unpleasant dreams, and in the morning they awake unrefreshed. When this practice is followed, the digestive organs lose their natural vigor, and the person finds himself a miserable dyspeptic."[14] *Dyspeptic* was a common nineteenth-century term for someone suffering from indigestion.

Eating a heavy meal late often disturbs our sleep. A Harvard School of Public Health report revealed that a lack of sleep could be a major contributor to the obesity epidemic.

"A good night's sleep is one of the keys to good health—and may also be a key to maintaining a healthy weight. There is mounting evidence that people who get too little sleep have a higher risk of weight gain and obesity than people who get seven to eight hours of sleep a night. Given our society's increasing tendency to burn the midnight oil—in 1998, 35 percent of American adults were getting 8 hours of sleep a night, and by 2005 that had dropped to 26 percent—lack of sleep could be a major contributor to the obesity epidemic."[15]

Many people ask, "Is it possible to get a balanced diet with only a light supper?" Actually, in planning a balanced diet, many people can do well nutritionally by eating a wide variety of fruits, nuts, grains, and vegetables **twice a day.** However, others may need **three meals** a day to maintain their ideal weight.

Ellen White wrote, "In most cases, two meals a day are preferable to three. Supper, when taken at an early hour, interferes with the digestion of the previous meal. When taken later, it is not itself digested before bedtime. Thus the stomach fails of securing proper rest. The sleep is disturbed, the brain and nerves are wearied, the appetite for breakfast is impaired, the whole system is unrefreshed, and is unready for the day's duties."[16]

The most practical plan is to **eat a large breakfast—like a king might eat,** a well-balanced **dinner in the middle of the day—like a prince might eat,** and a **light supper—the amount a pauper might have.** The lightest meal should be in the evening. Interestingly enough, this is **one of the best ways to control the overwhelming obesity and overweight problem worldwide.** So let's discuss one of the most serious health problems we are faced with.

5. WHAT IS A PRACTICAL WAY TO CONTROL OUR WEIGHT THROUGH OUR CHOICE OF FOODS?

The **benefits of a plant-based diet** consisting of vegetables, fruits, whole grains, and nuts are being confirmed by various studies as one of the best ways to control weight, in part from the physical properties of the foods themselves.

"Some foods—vegetables, nuts, fruits, and whole grains—were associated with less weight gain when consumption was actually increased. Obviously, such foods provide calories and cannot violate thermodynamic laws. Their inverse associations with weight gain suggest that the increase in their consumption reduced the intake of other foods to a greater (caloric) extent, decreasing the overall amount of energy consumed. Higher fiber content and slower digestion of these foods would augment satiety, and their increased consumption would also displace other, more highly processed foods in the diet, providing plausible biologic mechanisms whereby persons who eat more fruits, nuts, vegetables, and whole grains would gain less weight over time."[17]

WEIGHT CONTROL—A LIFESTYLE, NOT A RADICAL DIET

Reducing obesity is not dependent on a short-term fad diet. Radical approaches to weight control are typically unsustainable. It is far more sensible to take a balanced approach. In most cases, achieving our optimum weight is a matter of choosing a healthier, more positive lifestyle.

The key is not only to lose weight, but to keep it off. Remember the simple rule we discussed earlier: If you eat more calories than you burn up, then you gain weight. If you eat fewer calories than you burn, you lose weight. **If you want to lose weight without always feeling hungry, then eat high-fiber foods.**

6. HOW MANY CALORIES SHOULD AN AVERAGE MAN OR WOMAN BETWEEN THE AGES OF THIRTY AND SIXTY CONSUME?

MEN _____

WOMEN _____

The chart below lists the various calorie requirements for different age and activity groups.[18] Typically, a moderately active middle-aged male needs 2,400–2,600 calories a day while a moderately active middle-aged female needs approximately 2,000 calories a day.

Listed are the estimated number of calories needed to maintain the energy balance for various gender and age groups at three different levels of physical activity. The estimates are rounded to the nearest 200 calories and were determined using the Institute of Medicine equation.

Gender	Age (years)	Sedentary	Moderately Active	Active
Child	2–3	1,000	1,000–1,400	1,000–1,400
Female	4–8	1,200	1,400–1,600	1,400–1,800
	9–13	1,600	1,600–2,000	1,800–2,200
	14–18	1,800	2,000	2,400
	19–30	2,000	2,000–2,200	2,400
	31–50	1,800	2,000	2,200
	51+	1,600	1,800	2,000–2,200
Male	4–8	1,400	1,400–1,600	1,600–2,000
	9–13	1,800	1,800–2,200	2,000–2,600
	14–18	2,200	2,400–2,800	2,800–3,200
	19–30	2,400	2,600–2,800	3,000
	31–50	2,200	2,400–2,600	2,800–3,000
	51+	2,000	2,200–2,400	2,400–2,800

Eating good nutritious food and consuming the right amount of calories will help us maintain our weight. Here are some tips on weight control.

TIPS ON WEIGHT CONTROL

- **Make permanent lifestyle changes; weight loss is not a quick fix.**
  - **Choose** to make positive lifestyle choices.

- **Set** goals and take control.

- **Share** your goals with family members and friends.

• **Be determined and disciplined.**

- **Adopt** a plant-based diet as much as possible.

• **Eat at the right times.**

- Never or very rarely eat between meals.

- Make breakfast the best meal of the day.

- Eat a nutritious, well-balanced dinner, and eat a light supper. (Calories you eat at night are not all used up while you sleep.)

• **Eat foods higher in nutrients, especially high-fiber foods.**

- High-fiber foods are lower in calories, and they are filling and satisfying.

• **Avoid processed foods.**

- Keep your kitchen stocked with **"live" (natural)** foods not **"dead" (processed)** ones.

- Remember, the **best diet plan is to eat an abundance of fruits, vegetables, grains, and nuts in as natural a state as possible.**

• **Avoid empty calories.**

- Cut out or at least reduce sugar.

- Eliminate sugary drinks. Small amounts of sugar in soft drinks, coffee, and tea add up quickly throughout the day.

- Remember that diet drinks are not "something better."

- Eat only enough of the good calorie foods to maintain your ideal body weight. Be temperate.

• **Eat healthy home-cooked meals.**

- Eating out—especially at **all-you-can-eat** restaurants—does not help those who have difficulty controlling their appetites. Take smaller portions.

- Try the many options **in the** *Natural Lifestyle Cooking* **cookbook for good home-cooked meals.**

• **Plan your meals and menus.**

- Don't shop on an empty stomach.

- Stock your cupboards with all the necessary staples. The **shopping list in the appendix** will help you supply all the ingredients you need to make the recipes in the *Natural Lifestyle Cooking* cookbook.

- Before going to the grocery store, **make a shopping list** to help avoid impulse buying of unhealthful foods.

- **Cut out the unhealthy fast foods.**
  - "In 2001, Americans spent $110 billion on fast food, up nearly twentyfold in just three decades."[19]
  - Fast foods usually tend to be unhealthy. There are very few nutritious ones, so choose wisely.
- **Eat slowly to reduce the tendency to overeat.**
  - Chew your food thoroughly. Satisfaction from eating largely comes from the amount of time we chew our food.
  - Our bodies were designed by a loving Creator to chew our food thoroughly to facilitate digestion.
- **Drink plenty of pure water.**
  - Thirst can often be confused with hunger. Drinking water instead of eating in between meals will help you avoid consuming those extra calories. Someone has called water "the no calorie wonder."
- **Exercise more.**
  - **"Just do it."** A healthy weight-control program is incomplete without a good exercise routine.
  - Mix cardio with weight training. This is the best way to lose weight. Of course, there are lots of great fitness programs out there. Find one that you like best. Remember to bring your water bottle. Walking, of course, is an exercise that most people can do regularly. Plan to **walk** for **at least twenty to thirty minutes each day.**
  - Find a companion who will exercise with you. This always helps!
- **Get seven to eight hours of sleep.**
  - Without adequate sleep, it's harder to be disciplined to eat right and exercise.
  - Go to bed early. Remember, "Early to bed, early to rise, makes one healthy, wealthy, and wise." You will make much better choices if you get a good night's sleep.

REMEMBER, BALANCE IS THE KEY.

- **BE BALANCED** and reasonable in everything.
- **EAT MODERATELY** and temperately.
- **PLAN** for healthy treats occasionally.
- **ASK** God to help you. The One who made you will empower you to make positive choices and enable you to be in optimum health.

Supper Options

BEVERAGES

Many people include an alcoholic beverage with the evening meal as a way of relaxing from the stress of the day. Recent studies suggest that the health hazards of consuming alcoholic beverages far outweigh the attraction of their stress reduction. In the study done by Dr. Lester Breslow on the seven basic guidelines to increase life expectancy, one of the principles was to limit or eliminate completely the use of alcohol.[20] We would encourage you to avoid alcohol altogether. The U.S. Department of Health and Human Services, the National Institutes of Health, and the National Institute on Alcohol Abuse and Alcoholism make this thought-provoking observation:

> Clearly, alcohol affects the brain. Some of these impairments are detectable after only one or two drinks and quickly resolved when drinking stops. On the other hand, a person who drinks heavily over a long period of time may have brain deficits that persist well after he or she achieves sobriety. Exactly how alcohol affects the brain and the likelihood of reversing the impact of heavy drinking on the brain remain hot topics in alcohol research today.
>
> We do know that heavy drinking may have extensive and far-reaching effects on the brain, ranging from simple "slips" in memory to permanent and debilitating conditions that require lifetime custodial care. And even moderate drinking leads to short-term impairment, as shown by extensive research on the impact of drinking on driving.[21]

ALCOHOL CONSUMPTION AND CANCER RISK

Throughout these classes we have been learning how to reduce chronic diseases. Let's take a look at how eliminating alcohol not only improves your brain function, but can also reduce the risk of cancer.

"Heavy alcohol consumption increases the risk of human cancers of the mouth, throat, esophagus, liver, breast, and rectum.

"Even moderate alcohol use can raise the risk of some of these cancers. For example, in a study of over 7,000 women, as little as *three drinks per week* increased the risk of *breast cancer*. The more the person drank, the greater the risk."[22]

Some people counter with the question, "What about some of the research that seems to indicate alcohol is beneficial to the heart?" Neil Nedley reports, "Although widely touted for its heart benefits, alcohol is *clearly linked to several heart problems.* Both chronic heavy drinkers and those who become acutely intoxicated run the risk of heart rhythm disturbances. Cardiac arrhythmias, as they are called, can be as minor as a vague fluttering sensation in the chest or as major as sudden death. In fact, the high rate of sudden death among heavy alcohol users is likely due in part to these dangerous rhythm disturbances."[23]

Dr. Nedley continues, "Cardiomyopathy is another dangerous and sometimes fatal heart condition which is linked to alcohol use. Cardiomyopathy literally means 'heart muscle disease.' I have seen many patients whose heart muscles do not work as hard as they should because of alcohol consumption. . . . Although coronary artery disease can cause heart attacks and subsequent cardiomyopathy, current estimates are that 20 to 30 percent of all cardiomyopathy in our country is due to alcohol alone."[24]

Others might ask, "What about the beneficial antioxidants found in red wine?" "Dr. Demrow and colleagues at the University of Wisconsin looked directly at the constituents of red wine, white wine, and juice made from red grapes."[25] The results were fascinating. **It is not the alcohol in the wine, but the flavonoids in the grapes that are heart healthy.** "If it was not the alcohol, what are the substances that made the difference in the effects of the red wine and the grape juice? The most likely candidates were a group of substances called *flavonoids* that are known to prevent platelet clumping. They are found abundantly in grapes, red grape juice, and red wine."[26] The health benefit found in red wine is also found in **grapes and grape juice, but without the health hazards contained in the alcohol.**

" 'Researchers agree almost universally that no one should take up drinking for the express purpose of staving off heart disease . . . there are much safer and generally more healthful ways to protect the cardiovascular system.' "[27]

I believe we have had good advice from the researchers. Get the health benefit directly from the grapes the way God intended for us to get it.

White and red 100 percent pure grape juice

Martha Grogan, a Mayo Clinic cardiologist, says, "Keep in mind that it's also beneficial to eat whole grapes—not just grape juice. Some research suggests that whole grapes deliver the same amount of antioxidants that are in grape juice and wine but have the added benefit of providing dietary fiber."[28]

A study led by Keith Singletary, PhD, professor of nutrition at the University of Illinois at Urbana-Champaign, and lead author of the study, found that purple grapes may have some cancer-fighting properties. "These studies indicate that components of Concord grape juice can inhibit the growth of certain types of breast cancer cells in rats."[29] Singletary adds that while these findings are preliminary and based on animal-model research, they certainly suggest the need to look more closely at the possible benefits that Concord grape juice may offer women.

Many people who are trying to control their weight would do great with just **nutritious, delicious beverages at suppertime.** Let's take a look at some healthy ones.

Although there are some people who may prefer to eat just two meals a day, there are others who could use a few more calories in the evening. Why not try a **nutritious, delicious treat** of a **PIÑA COLADA** or a **STRAWBERRY-TOFU-ALMOND SMOOTHIE**?

Piña Colada

1 ½ c. crushed pineapple with juice
1 c. coconut soy ice cream
½ c. coconut milk
Cream of coconut

BLEND and SERVE.

Delicious **PIÑA COLADA**

Strawberry-Tofu-Almond Smoothie

1 c. soymilk	2 c. frozen strawberries
4 dates, pitted	1 c. frozen pineapple
1 apple	chunks
6 almonds	1 c. frozen peach slices
½ c. Silken tofu (firm)	1 c. frozen mango
	chunks

BLEND soymilk, dates, apple, nuts, and tofu until smooth. ADD remaining fruit and BLEND well.

SMOOTHIES

A **fruit smoothie** is a blended beverage made from fresh or frozen fruit. In addition to fruit, many smoothies include crushed ice. They can also be made with fresh juices or soymilk/nut milk. Smoothies became widely available in the United States in the late 1960s when ice-cream vendors and health-food stores began selling them. By the 1990s, smoothies became available in many places including shopping malls, supermarkets, and even airports. They are extremely popular now. There are more smoothie shops springing up all the time. Smoothies are easy to make and can be nutritious. An incentive to make your own homemade smoothies is that they are not filled with sugary syrup. Choose the kind of fruit you like, blend it with a little fresh juice, and you will have a delicious drink. Use a little creativity in your smoothie making and develop your own fruit blend. You will enjoy this special treat.

7. WHAT IS A HEALTHY ALTERNATIVE TO COFFEE AND TEA?

A. _____

B. _____

Coffee substitutes are caffeine-free products made from roasted grain. The first cereal coffee in the United States began with **Postum**®, made from roasted grains and molasses. This healthy alternative to coffee goes back to 1895, when C. W. Post created this beverage from a recipe used by John Harvey Kellogg in the Battle Creek Sanitarium. Post learned about cereal coffee while he was a patient at the Battle Creek Sanitarium, which was a world-renowned health institution in the late nineteenth and early twentieth century. He formed the Postum Cereal Company to manufacture and sell Postum Food Coffee. This beverage became very popular during World War II, when real coffee was being rationed. As a coffee substitute, it was endorsed as a healthier option to coffee without any of the side effects. Now that the production of Postum has been discontinued, other cereal coffee substitutes have flooded the market. Some of the readily available ones are Pero® and Roma®.

Healthful beverages are a great option for weight watchers or people who just simply want to eat light in the evening.

For people who need something a little more substantial than a hot beverage or a smoothie for supper, we will discuss a few more options.

8. WHAT ARE SOME OTHER SIMPLE SUPPER OPTIONS?

A. _____

B. _____

C. _____

Fresh fruit is a wonderful option for a light supper.

Fruit in Orange Juice

3 peaches, peeled and sliced

1 c. strawberries, hulled and sliced

½ c. blueberries

2 bananas, sliced

1 c. orange juice

MIX and SERVE.

BREADS · GRAINS

9. WHAT IS ONE OF THE MOST EASILY DIGESTIBLE FOODS THAT IS GREAT FOR SUPPER?

   ZWIEBACK is a great food for supper. It is one of the **most easily digestible** foods to eat. Zwieback is simply twice-baked bread.

   Ellen White, an eighteenth-century health promoter, stated, "Crackers—the English biscuit—or zwieback, and fruit, or cereal coffee, are the foods best suited for the evening meal."[30]

Cereal coffee beverage with **CRISPY OAT CAKES** or **ZWIEBACK**

Zwieback

8 slices of whole-grain bread

BAKE at about 175° to 200°F for 2 to 3 hours, until all the moisture has evaporated. It will be lightly brown.

Popcorn is another good choice for supper. You may want to substitute it for bread in the evening. Just be careful about the butter and salt you add. You may want to try adding a little nutritional yeast. Popcorn with a little nutritional yeast mixed in makes it more nutritious, and it actually enhances the flavor.

Here is the key to healthy suppers. Keep it simple. Rather than eating a large meal in the evening, reduce the amount you eat. Focus on fruit, a slice of whole-grain bread, or a delicious smoothie. This is a great way to start on the road to better health. Eating simple at night after having a substantial breakfast and a well-balanced dinner is a great beginning to help improve your health. **Remember, lifestyle is the key to living a longer, healthier, happier life.** Start today by choosing a way of life that will keep you healthy.

ANSWERS FOR CLASS 5

1. A. PHYSICAL   Better weight control; healthier eating habits
   B. MENTAL   Better academic performance
   C. SOCIAL   Better communication skills
   D. BEHAVIORAL   Less substance abuse, less theft, less disordered and high-risk
                      eating behaviors
   E. SPIRITUAL   Better and stronger faith

2. A. Obese—35.9 percent
   B. Overweight—33.3 percent
   C. Total—69.2 percent

3. A. Eating too many calories
   B. Too little physical activity

4. A. Eat fewer calories
   B. Exercise more
   C. Eat a lighter supper and larger breakfast

5. Timing of meals; eating nothing in between meals

6. A. Men—2,200 to 2,500 daily (more if active)
   B. Women—1,800 to 2,200 (more if active)

7. A. Cereal coffee without caffeine
   B. Herbal teas

8. A. Fruit
   B. Whole grains
   C. Simple soups

9. Zwieback

ENDNOTES

1. "In U.S., Majority Overweight or Obese in All 50 States," accessed April 22, 2013, http://www.gallup.com/poll/156707/majority-overweight-obese-states.aspx.

2. Gary L. Hopkins, Duane, McBride, Shelley Bacon, Daniel D. Saugh, and Julie Westlake, "Eat Together, Live Well Together," *Adventist Review* (October 2011): 19; see also Shira Feldman, Marla E. Eisenberg, Diane Neumark-Sztainer, and Mary Story, "Associations Between Watching TV During Family Meals and Dietary Intake Among Adolescents," *Journal of Nutrition Education and Behavior* 39, no. 5 (September/October 2010): 257–263.

3. Hopkins, 19; see also Jayne A. Fulkerson, Martha Y. Kubik, Mary Story, L. Lytle, and Chrisa Arcan, "Are There Nutritional and Other Benefits Associated With Family Meals Among At-Risk Youth?" *Journal of Adolescent Health* 45, no. 4 (October 2009): 389–395.

4. Hopkins, 20; see also Council of Economic Advisers, "Teens and Their Parents in the Twenty-First Century: An Examination of the Trends in Teen Behavior and the Role of Parental Involvement," November 18, 2010, http://clinton3.nara.gov/WH/EOP/CEA/html/Teens_Paper_Final.pdf.

5. Hopkins, 21; see also National Center on Addiction and Substance Abuse at Columbia University, "The Importance of Family Dinners IV," September 20, 2007, accessed November 18, 2010, http://www.casacolumbia.org/templates/PressReleases.aspx?articleid=502&zoneid=65.

6. Hopkins, 20; see also James White and Emma Halliwell, "Alcohol and Tobacco Use During Adolescence: The Importance of the Family Mealtime Environment," *Journal of Health Psychology* 15, no. 4 (May 2010): 526–532.

7. Hopkins, 20; see also Bisakha Sen, "The Relationship Between Frequency of Family Dinner and Adolescent Problem Behaviors After Adjusting for Other Family Characteristics," *Journal of Adolescence* 33, no. 1 (February 2010): 187–196.

8. Hopkins, 20; see also Council of Economic Advisers, "Teens and Their Parents in the Twenty-First Century."

9. Hopkins, 21; see also Search Institute, "Effective Christian Education: A National Study of Protestant Congregations," 1990.

10. World Health Organization, "Unhealthy Diets and Physical Inactivity," accessed May 6, 2013, http://www.who.int/nmh/publications/fact_sheet_diet_en.pdf.

11. "Study: American Obesity Epidemic Much Worse Than CDC Believes," accessed April 22, 2013, http://www.USNews.com/news/articles/2012/04/02/study-american-obesity-epidemic-much-worse-than-cdc-believes; "Is Obesity a Bigger Problem

Than We Thought?" accessed April 22, 2013, http://www.youbeauty.com/body-fitness/obesity-diagnosis.

12.   "By 2020 75 Percent of America Will Be Obese," accessed May 22, 2013, www.newsmax.com/newsfront/202075
-percentamerica-obese/2010/09/23/id/371359.

13.   "Genes Are Not Destiny," accessed April 22, 2013, http://www.hsph.harvard.edu/obesity-prevention-source/obesity
-causes/genes-and-obesity/.

14.   Ellen G. White, *Christian Temperance and Bible Hygiene,* online edition (Silver Spring, Md.: Ellen G. White Estate, 2010), 50.

15.   "Sleep," accessed January 23, 2013, http://www.hsph.harvard.edu/obesity-prevention-source/obesity-causes/sleep-and
-obesity/.

16.   White, *Counsels on Diets and Foods,* 176.

17.   "Changes in Diet and Lifestyle and Long-Term Weight Gain in Women and Men," *New England Journal of Medicine,*
accessed April 22, 2013, http://www.nejm.org/doi/full/10.1056/NEJMoa1014296.

18.   Kathleen M. Zelman, "Weight Loss and Diet Plans," WebMD, http://www.webmd.com/diet/features/estimated-calorie
-requirement.

19.   "Why People Become Overweight," accessed March 19, 2013, http://www.health.harvard.edu/newsweek/why-people
-become-overweight.html.

20.   "Seven Secrets to a Long Life," accessed June 12, 2013, http://www.berkshirepublishing.com/ans/htmview
.asp?paritem=s031000342a.

21.   The U.S. Department of Health and Human Services, the National Institutes of Health, and the National Institute on Alcohol
Abuse and Alcoholism, Document 63, "Alcohol's Damaging Effects on the Brain" (2004).

22.   Neil Nedley, *Proof Positive,* 431; italics in original; see also K. J. Isselbacher et al., *Harrison's Principles of Internal Medicine,*
13th ed. (N.Y.: McGraw-Hill, 1994), CD-ROM version; W. N. Kelly et al., *Textbook of Internal Medicine,* 2nd ed. (Philadelphia, Pa.:
J. P. Lippincott, 1992); U.S. Department of Health and Human Services, "Effects of Alcohol on Health and Body Systems," *Eighth
Special Report to the US Congress on Alcohol and Health,* National Institutes of Health Publication No. 94-3699, (September
1993): 177, 178; A. Schatzkin et al., "Alcohol Consumption and Breast Cancer in the Epidemiology Follow-up Study of the First
National Health and Nutrition Examination Survey," *New England Journal of Medicine* 316, no. 19 (May 7, 1987): 1169–1173.

23.   Nedley, 433; italics in original; see also U.S. Department of Health and Human Services, "Effects of Alcohol on Health and
Body Systems," 174, 175.

24.   Nedley.

25.   Nedley, 443; see also H. S. Demrow, P. R. Slane, J. D. Folts, "Administration of Wine and Grape Juice Inhibits In Vivo
Platelet Activity and Thrombosis in Stenosed Canine Coronary Arteries," *Circulation* 91, no. 4 (February 15, 1995): 1182–1188.

26.   Nedley, 444; italics in original.

27.   Tufts University, "Special Report: Uncorking the Facts About Alcohol and Your Health," Tufts University Diet and Nutrition
Letter 13, no. 6 (August 1995): 4–6, cited in ibid., 446.

28.   Martha Grogan, "Grape Juice: Same Heart Benefits as Wine?" Mayo Clinic, accessed May 7, 2013, http://www.Mayoclinic
.com/health/food-and-nutrition/an00576.

29.   Accessed May 7, 2013, http://www.researchgate.net/publication/8988544_Inhibition_of_rat_mammary_tumorigenesis
_by_concord_grape_juice_constituents.

30.   White, *Counsels on Diet and Foods,* 431, 432.

Class 6

Holidays and Special Occasions

Holidays · Hospitality

For most people, holidays and special occasions are happy times when we especially enjoy our family and friends. There is something special about having our loved ones and close friends visit our homes. But it does take a lot of effort to prepare for these occasions. We spend hours shopping, preparing, cooking, and cleaning up. Then in just a very short time, the day is over. Was it worth all the effort? Certainly! The enjoyment we share and the memories we build are worth every ounce of energy we expend. If the meals we prepare serve much more than simply enjoyment for the moment—if they serve a double purpose—we, too, will be doubly blessed. **Nutritious meals provide not only immediate joy, but they also promote long-term health.**

Because the focus on holidays is so often on eating, why not **select foods that are both tasty and healthy.** Many of the **dishes prepared for the holidays contain many calories and few nutrients.** This causes a tendency to overeat, resulting in those undesirable pounds. I know many people say, "Oh well, I will go on a diet after the holidays," or "I will eat healthier after the party." The good news is **we can celebrate holidays, birthdays, and other special occasions with delicious, health-giving, and satisfying food.** On holidays, why not give your family and friends the special gift of great-tasting, nutritious, colorful food?

1. **LIST SEVEN PRINCIPLES THAT WILL HELP YOUR FAMILY HAVE HEALTHY HOLIDAYS.**

    1. _____

    2. _____

    3. _____

    4. _____

    5. _____

    6. _____

    7. _____

The key to a healthy lifestyle is balance. Balance necessitates making wise choices and being temperate in all things. One side of the coin of temperance is to abstain from everything that is harmful, such as drugs, alcohol, tobacco, and foods and beverages that are detrimental to our health. The other side of the coin is to eat nutritious, healthful foods in moderation. Overeating on even good foods can negatively affect our health. A good principle to follow is to eat moderately, especially around the holidays. Eating moderately may mean saying, "No, thank you," to that second piece of dessert. To really enjoy a healthy lifestyle, we must also keep moving. Exercise is another important key to good health. It takes discipline, but it will pay off in the end. After eating a heavier-than-usual holiday meal, why not invite the entire family out for a long walk in the fresh air. Another key to good health is positive relationships with the people around us. Enjoy relationships. Making our family and friends a priority builds healthy relationships that are critical to good health. Several hugs a day go a long way toward building long and lasting relationships. Be sure to do something nice for others around you. We are the ones who receive the greatest blessing when we surprise someone else with a random act of kindness. Remember, a thankful heart and an attitude of gratitude is life giving. Be thankful for the abundance of good things God has given you. Be thankful you can improve your health by following God's health principles. "Be thankful to Him, and bless His name. For the LORD is good" (Psalm 100:4, 5).

Holidays

THANKSGIVING

For most Americans, Thanksgiving is a holiday they especially enjoy. It is a time to reflect on the past year and be thankful for the blessings of life. Let's take a look at how the Thanksgiving holiday was established. The Pilgrims emigrated from England to Holland and later sailed to America, where they anchored their ship the *Mayflower* at the tip of Cape Cod in Provincetown Harbor, Massachusetts. They settled at what they called Plymouth Plantation. Those who survived that first winter were thankful and rejoiced in the good harvest of crops. In the autumn of 1621, the Pilgrims, along with the Wampanoag Indians, shared a great harvest feast, which is traditionally known as the first Thanksgiving. The celebration lasted three days. On November 26, 1789, George Washington, first president of the United States, proclaimed the first nationwide Thanksgiving celebration in America. It was to be a national day of thanksgiving and prayer to be observed by gratefully acknowledging the blessings of God. However, some people were opposed to such a holiday. It wasn't until 1863 that President Abraham Lincoln proclaimed the last Thursday in November as a national day of thanksgiving. Every president after Lincoln continued the Thanksgiving holiday. Although the actual date in November was changed a few times, it was on December 26, 1941, that President Franklin D. Roosevelt signed a bill into law making the fourth Thursday in November a national holiday. The bill was finally passed by Congress as a legal Thanksgiving holiday.

Thanksgiving is a wonderful time to reflect on God's blessings on our lives just as those first Pilgrims did on that New England Thanksgiving so long ago. It is a day when many Americans gather together with their families and loved ones. It is also a day to invite friends and those who may not have families or any place to go for dinner to enjoy a nutritious meal and a warm family atmosphere. However, an attitude of gratitude is something we should cultivate every day. Many documented studies prove that **gratitude and thankfulness** are major factors in promoting better health and making people feel better about their own lives. Interestingly, grateful people also exercise more.

"Two psychologists, Dr. Robert A. Emmons of the University of California, Davis, and Dr. Michael E. McCullough of the University of Miami, have done much of the research on gratitude. In one study, they asked all participants to write a few sentences each week, focusing on particular topics. One group wrote about things they were grateful for that had occurred during the week. A second group wrote about daily irritation or things that had displeased them (with no emphasis on their being positive or negative). After 10 weeks, those who wrote about gratitude were more optimistic and felt better about their lives. Surprisingly, they also exercised more and had fewer visits to physicians than those who focused on sources of aggravation."[1]

Thankfulness helps improve the immune system. Grateful people seem to take a greater interest in their health. We can boost our immune system by our lifestyle practices. According to Dr. Emmons's research on gratitude, "Grateful people take better care of themselves and engage in more protective health behaviors like regular exercise, a healthy diet, regular physical examinations."[2]

One of the most important choices we can make each day is the choice to have a positive attitude. A new study reported by researchers from the University of Kansas found that positive emotions are critical to maintaining physical health for people worldwide. "There is a science that is emerging that says a positive attitude isn't just a state of mind. It also has linkages to what's going on in the brain and in the body."[3]

Gratitude and thanksgiving in all of life's circumstances are two of the most powerful health-giving emotions. Is it possible to cultivate a positive spirit and attitude of thanksgiving in even very difficult circumstances? Read what Matthew Henry entered in his diary after he was robbed: "I have so much to be thankful for: I am thankful that God wrought such a change in my heart that it was I who was being robbed, and not the one doing the robbing. I am thankful that even though the young man took my money, he did not take my life also. I am thankful that even though he took my money bag there wasn't much inside of it. I am thankful that I alone was injured and not any additional persons. I am thankful that my life is so much more than the earthly possessions God has granted to me in my sojourn here, and I am thankful that even should I have lost my life in this encounter I know heaven is awaiting me, where the riches of God's glory far outweigh the total of all man's riches."[4]

There is a song of thankfulness that we have often sung before meals. It goes like this:

"There is so much for which to be thankful;

there are gifts so abundant each day,

so we thank thee, dear Lord for thy mercies

that attend us along life's way."

Along with you, I desire to learn the art of being thankful each day. Thankfulness can actually improve our immune system. Why not choose to be more thankful every day? That brings us to a very important subject: the **immune system.** Let's explore what the immune system is, its importance, and how to make it stronger.

THE IMMUNE SYSTEM

2.   WHAT IS THE IMMUNE SYSTEM?

The **immune system is a system of biological structures and processes within an organism that protects against disease.** To function properly, an immune system must detect a wide variety of agents, from viruses to parasitic worms, and distinguish them from the organism's own healthy tissue. In essence, it is the bodily system that protects the body from disease or foreign substances. Researchers are still studying the intricacies of the immune system, including exploring the effects of diet and exercise. The one major line of defense to boost the immune system is a healthy lifestyle. Harvard University Medical School Health Publications made this fascinating observation:

"A different scientific approach looks at the effect of certain lifestyle modifications on the incidence of disease. If a study shows significantly less disease, researchers consider whether the immune system is being strengthened in some way. Based on these studies, there is now evidence that even though we may not be able to prove a direct link between a certain lifestyle and an improved immune response, we can at least show that some links are likely."[5]

3.   WHAT IS THE BEST WAY TO KEEP YOUR IMMUNE SYSTEM STRONG AND HEALTHY?

Harvard Medical School Publications, in an article on how to boost your immune system, stated, "Following general good-health guidelines is the single best step you can take toward keeping your immune system strong and healthy. Every part of your body, including your immune system, functions better when protected from environmental assaults and bolstered by healthy-living strategies such as these:

- Don't smoke
- Eat a diet high in fruits, vegetables, and whole grains, and low in saturated fat.

- Exercise regularly.
- Maintain a healthy weight.
- Control your blood pressure.
- If you drink alcohol, drink only in moderation. [Our advice is to eliminate it all together.]
- Get adequate sleep.
- Take steps to avoid infection, such as washing your hands frequently and cooking meats thoroughly. [Of course, a plant-based diet is the best choice.]
- Get regular medical screening tests for people in your age group and risk category."[6]

BOOSTING THE IMMUNE SYSTEM

It is amazing that the **natural laws of health** we are promoting in our classes are the very laws science is confirming today. God's natural laws of health are the true remedies for staying healthy. Ellen White, a health educator, wrote as early as 1905, "Pure air, sunlight, abstemiousness, rest, exercise, proper diet, the use of water, trust in divine power—these are the true remedies. Every person should have a knowledge of nature's remedial agencies and how to apply them."[7]

These laws of health will help keep us strong and healthy. They work in harmony with one another. It takes all eight lifestyle practices to achieve optimum health. These principles of health are so important that we have an entire section called **"Eight Natural Lifestyle Secrets"** in the *Natural Lifestyle Cooking* cookbook on pages 173–189.

When it comes to diet, researchers are investigating the immune-boosting potential of a number of different nutrients; but one thing is sure, if you eat a wide variety of fruits, nuts, grains, and vegetables, you will get the essential nutrients for good health. However, listed here are a few of the essential nutrients to help boost our immune systems:

- SELENIUM is a mineral that is an important nutrient vital to the functioning of the immune system. It works with vitamins such as E and C to help prevent free radical damage in the body. Some studies have suggested that people with low selenium levels are at greater risk of bladder, breast, colon, rectum, lung, and prostate cancers. Let's look at just a few foods for Thanksgiving that are high in selenium. Brazil nuts are at the top of the list, so be sure to include them with that bowl of mixed nuts on your Thanksgiving table. Wheat germ and oats are also high; so how about serving APPLE CRISP on page 44 of the *Natural Lifestyle Cooking* cookbook?

- VITAMIN A is an important nutrient for maintaining a strong immune system. Vitamin A deficiency is associated with impaired immunity and increased risk of infectious disease. Foods high in vitamin A are sweet potatoes, carrots, butternut squash, red and green leaf lettuce, and dried apricots. There are recipes in the *Natural Lifestyle Cooking* cookbook using all these ingredients, including a nutritious and delicious **CARROT PIE** filled with vitamin A, which is found on page 160. Oh, by the way, there's no sugar in the pie. It has only a natural sweetener of dates. Try it. It is one of our favorite desserts.

- **VITAMIN C** works in concert with other micronutrients, such as vitamin E and selenium. Some plant foods high in vitamin C are oranges, strawberries, kiwis, broccoli, and cauliflower. A delightful nutritious fruit plate or raw vegetable platter is always a hit on the holidays. A scrumptious **RELISH TRAY** is pictured in the cookbook on page 104.

- **VITAMIN D** is an important vitamin. The preponderance of scientific research indicates that this important nutrient is essential for a strong immune system. Vitamin D is produced when skin is exposed to sunlight. It has been known that people afflicted with tuberculosis respond well to sunlight. We can get vitamin D with fortified soymilk and tofu as well as adequate sunshine. Orange juice and other fortified foods are a good way to get vitamin D. Some people feel the necessity of supplementing their diets with moderate amounts of vitamin D. If you choose a vitamin D supplement, be sure to consult with your primary care physician first.

- **VITAMIN E** works in concert with vitamin C and selenium to help boost the immune system. Foods high in vitamin E are sunflower seeds, almonds, pine nuts, and dried apricots. **APRICOT JAM** is wonderful to spread over homemade dinner rolls for the Thanksgiving holiday. These are just a few of the essential nutrients to boost the immune system and you can get them all, even on the holidays.

Along with a thankful heart, choose a healthy, nutritious diet this Thanksgiving. Notice that one of the lifestyle practices to build the immune system is to eat a diet high in fruits, vegetables, and whole grains. You can make healthy choices and easily modify the typical Thanksgiving dinner just a little bit and make it quite healthy.

NEW ENGLANDERS' TRADITIONAL FOODS AT THANKSGIVING

The nutritious bounties of the harvest that the Pilgrims ate are still Thanksgiving favorites today. What are some of the **traditional foods that New Englanders still enjoy at Thanksgiving?** The top ten traditional Thanksgiving dishes are **turkey (vege-turkey or HOLIDAY ROAST** for those of us who are vegan vegetarians), **bread stuffing/dressing, mashed potatoes, butternut squash, sweet potatoes, green bean casserole, cranberry sauce, rolls/bread, pumpkin and apple pies.** As a child growing up in New England, these dishes were common in our home on Thanksgiving. This tradition continues in our family even today. Of course, we always add a colorful platter of fresh raw veggies. You will notice we exchanged the turkey for a vege-turkey dish. We have been learning in these classes why a plant-based diet is the best choice.

In addition to the apple and pumpkin pies for dessert, we always enjoy having **a bowl of mixed nuts still in their shells** on the dessert table. The sound of nuts cracking is part of our family tradition at Thanksgiving.

4. WHAT KIND OF NUTS ARE THE MOST BENEFICIAL TO OUR HEALTH?

Nuts such as almonds, Brazil nuts, pecans, and walnuts are the most nutritious. Studies indicate that nuts eaten in their natural state without oil and salt are the most beneficial. The additional salt has the potential of raising our blood pressure, and excessive oils may have a detrimental effect on our blood vessels. It is a good practice to include nuts in our dietary fare all year round. We make it a habit to eat nuts every day, and we use them in abundance in a variety of recipes at holiday times. If you haven't been eating many nuts, you might want to begin eating some today.

NUTRITIONAL BENEFITS OF NUTS:

- Nuts provide high levels of **protein.** Their protein content is usually greater than that of animal products.
- Nuts provide **vitamins and minerals.** They contain a host of **antioxidants.**
- Nuts provide an excellent source of **fiber.**
- Nuts provide **energy.** They give us natural needed calories.
- Nuts **contain no cholesterol** and are effective in reducing cholesterol levels.
- Nuts **protect the heart** by reducing the risk of coronary heart disease.

- Nuts are **not processed,** and they can be eaten raw.
- Nuts can be **used in cooking.** They are a healthful alternative to meat because of their high quality of protein.

A Harvard Health article in May 2005 titled, "Eating Nuts Promotes Cardiovascular Health," shares the great health value in nuts.

EATING NUTS PROMOTES CARDIOVASCULAR HEALTH

"Researchers from Harvard Medical School and the Harvard School of Public Health have examined the effect of eating nuts on cardiovascular health, reports the *Harvard Men's Health Watch*. 'Their work shows that nuts really are healthy, especially for men at risk for heart disease,' says Dr. Harvey B. Simon, editor. Studies show that healthy men, and those who have already suffered a heart attack, can reduce cardiovascular risk by eating nuts regularly. Doctors theorize that:

- nuts may help lower cholesterol, partly by replacing less healthy foods in the diet
- nuts contain mono- and polyunsaturated fats known to benefit the heart
- the omega-3 fats found in walnuts may protect against irregular heart rhythms
- nuts are rich in arginine, a substance that may improve blood vessel function
- other nutrients in nuts (such as fiber and vitamin E) may also help lower cardiovascular risk.

"Nuts are nutritional powerhouses, but high in calories. The *Harvard Men's Health Watch* cautions that if you add nuts to your diet, you'll want to cut back on something else. Substitute nuts for chips or cookies, and avoid nuts that are fried in oil or loaded with salt. As little as two ounces of nuts a week appears to help lower the risk of heart disease. Healthful choices include:

- almonds
- Brazil nuts
- cashews
- filberts
- peanuts
- pistachios
- walnuts

"By themselves, nuts seem to produce modest declines in cholesterol, but when they are combined with other healthful foods, the results can be spectacular. 'Nuts may not be the key to cardiovascular health, but adding nuts to a balanced, healthful diet can take you one step away from heart disease,' says Dr. Simon."[8]

BEST NUTS FOR HEALTH

Below are the USDA Nutrition Facts of some of the best nuts for our health.

- **ALMONDS** are high in protein, with 20 grams in 1 cup ground (95 grams). One cup is also filled with 12 grams of fiber, which is 46 percent of the daily value. Almonds are also a source of calcium. One cup contains 25 percent of the daily value. (Percent daily values are based on a 2,000-calorie diet. Your daily values may be higher or lower depending on your calorie needs.)[9]

- **BRAZIL NUTS** are high in selenium. "If it's selenium you're after—as many men are, because the mineral might protect against prostate cancer—then look to Brazil nuts: One ounce has almost 10 times the Recommended Dietary Allowance (RDA) of 55 micrograms."[10]

- **PECANS** are packed with many important nutrients such as vitamins A and C. Pecans contain calcium, iron, and other minerals such as potassium, magnesium, zinc, and selenium. They are also a natural source of high-quality protein with 10 grams of protein and 10 grams of fiber in approximately 1 cup, with no cholesterol.[11]

- **WALNUTS** contain 18 grams of protein and 8 grams of fiber per cup, chopped. They also contain omega-3 fatty acids. Walnuts contain 11 percent of our calcium daily requirements and 19 percent of the daily iron requirement.[12]

"Perhaps one of the most unexpected and novel findings in nutritional epidemiology in the past 5 years has been that nut consumption seems to protect against ischemic heart disease (IHD). The frequency and quantity of nut consumption have been documented to be higher in vegetarian than in non-vegetarian populations. Nuts also constitute an important part of other plant-based diets, such as Mediterranean and Asian diets. In a large, prospective epidemiologic study of Seventh-day Adventists in California, we found that frequency of nut consumption had a substantial and highly significant inverse association with risk of myocardial infarction and death from IHD. The Iowa Women's Health Study also documented an association between nut consumption and decreased risk of IHD. The protective effect of nuts on IHD has been found in men and women and in the elderly. Importantly, nuts have similar associations in both vegetarians and non-vegetarians. The protective effect of nut consumption on IHD is not offset by increased mortality from other causes. Moreover, frequency of nut consumption has been found to be inversely related to all-cause mortality in several population groups such as whites, blacks, and the elderly. Thus, nut consumption may not only offer protection against IHD, but also increase longevity."[13]

We often have a dish of raw walnuts, pecans, and almonds on the table at breakfast time, and I regularly use nuts in my cooking. Try adding nuts to your diet by **serving some delicious PECAN ROLLS and PECAN PIE.** Your family will enjoy PECAN ROLLS on holidays. I am including my recipes for nutritious PECAN ROLLS made with a mixture of whole grains and lots of pecans on the outside and for a nutritious PECAN PIE.

Try these delicious whole-wheat **PECAN ROLLS**. Pecans are filled with protein, fiber, vitamins, and minerals.

Pecan Rolls

¼ c. warm water
2 T. active dry yeast
1 ½ c. hot water
1 c. almond milk
½ c. brown sugar
1 T. salt
¼ c. light olive oil
½ c. wheat germ
1 c. quick oats
2 c. whole-wheat flour
1 c. barley flour
2 to 2 ½ c. enriched unbleached flour

MIX active yeast in ¼ cup warm water. **COMBINE** hot water, almond milk, brown sugar, salt, and oil. **STIR** in wheat germ, oats, whole-wheat flour, and barley flour. **STIR** in yeast mixture. **ADD** unbleached flour gradually to make moderately stiff dough. **TURN OUT** on a lightly floured surface. **KNEAD** until smooth and satiny. **SHAPE** dough into a ball. **PLACE** in lightly greased bowl. **COVER** and let rise in warm place until double (about 1 ½ hours). **PUNCH** down. **SHAPE** into rolls. **PLACE** rolls in muffin tin on top of the PECAN TOPPING. **LET RISE** until double (about 40 minutes). **BAKE** 30 to 35 minutes at 350°F.

Pecan Topping

3 T. corn syrup
2 T. brown sugar

⅓ c. Earth Balance® margarine
1 c. chopped pecans

MIX corn syrup, brown sugar, and margarine together in saucepan. **BRING** to a boil. **DIVIDE** chopped pecans equally among the muffin cups. **POUR** PECAN TOPPING over pecans in the muffin tin.

Pecan Pie

¼ c. brown sugar
⅔ c. maple syrup
¼ c. Earth Balance® margarine
¼ c. soymilk
6 oz. Silken tofu (firm)
2 T. cornstarch
½ t. salt
1 t. vanilla extract
2 c. pecans, chopped
¾ c. whole pecans (arranged on top)

CREAM the brown sugar, maple syrup, and margarine together. **BLEND** tofu in soymilk. **ADD** tofu to brown sugar mixture. **ADD** cornstarch, salt, and vanilla extract. **ADD** chopped pecans to the mixture. **POUR** into an unbaked wheat-germ pie crust. **ARRANGE** whole pecans on top. **BAKE** pie at 375°F for 40 to 45 minutes. **COOL** and **ENJOY.**

Holiday Roast

1 onion, chopped
1 c. celery, chopped
2 cloves garlic, minced
1 T. olive oil
1 lb. extra-firm tofu, mashed
1 ½ c. Cedar Lake® vegeburger
½ c. cashews, chopped fine
1 ½ c. bread stuffing
1 t. sage
1 T. McKay's® chicken-style seasoning
1 to 3 T. gluten flour

SAUTÉ onion, celery, and garlic in olive oil. **MIX** all ingredients together. **BAKE** at 350°F for 1 hour.

There are more holiday recipes in the *Natural Lifestyle Cooking* cookbook, such as the traditional New England **APPLE PIE** (page 159) and many more.

CHRISTMAS

It's beginning to look a lot like Christmas! Your house is decorated for the family and others to enjoy. The multicolored Christmas lights gladden our hearts while the familiar Christmas carols lift our spirits. The wrapped presents under the tree remind us of those we love. Christmas has a certain aroma. The smell of homemade bread, **PECAN ROLLS,** and **APPLE PIE** fill our home each Christmas season. The great joy of Christmas is being together with children, grandchildren, brothers, sisters, aunts, uncles, friends, and the people who mean the most to us. The holidays are joyous, festive occasions. It is the time of year that is **celebrated with family traditions.** It is a time of sharing gifts and participating in many pleasant family activities. One of the most enjoyable times is Christmas dinner. There is something warm and special about sitting around the Christmas table with the entire family. So, what's cooking in the kitchen? I'm sure your family will enjoy these healthful recipes at Christmas. Christmas may be the time to be jolly, but if we overeat unhealthful food and sugar-laden desserts, we may end up more fat than fit. What can you do to plan healthful meals for your family during this joyful time of year?

Remember that the true meaning of Christmas is the celebration of Jesus Christ's birth, **which has deep significance for Christians. Christmas is a time to share gifts with others**

APPLE PIE made from fresh McIntosh apples is regularly served at traditional New England Thanksgiving dinners. The recipe is in the *Natural Lifestyle Cooking* cookbook, page 159.

A nutritious Christmas dinner looks good and tastes good.

because God has given the greatest gift of all, Jesus. One of the best ways to celebrate the Christmas holidays is to **give to those in need.** One of the most satisfying Christmas activities is to help people in our communities who are less fortunate than we are. We can help them enjoy the Christmas holidays too. The spirit of Christmas is the spirit of giving. The joy of Christmas is the joy of sharing. In our family we like to reflect on what we can do to bless the lives of others and bring them cheer at Christmas. For years **I have baked loaves of whole-wheat and raisin bread to give to our friends, neighbors, and work associates at Christmas.** I wrap the loaves in silver foil and put a red or green bow on the top. At times we have distributed food baskets to people in need during the holiday season. You may want to discuss with your family what you can do to especially brighten someone else's holiday this year. It may be inviting a lonely widow over for Thanksgiving or Christmas dinner or possibly bringing a food basket, toys, or clothing to someone in need. This is the true spirit of the holidays. So make a beautiful food basket and give gifts to the children. You will be glad you did.

Relax and Enjoy the Christmas Holidays!

TIPS FOR HOLIDAY MEAL PLANNING

Planning holiday meals for family and friends can be lots of fun, but it can also be somewhat stressful. Here are some tips for taking the stress out of your holiday meal planning while at the same time serving nutritious and delicious meals for your family.

• **PLAN MENUS.** Stress-free holidays require careful planning. Whether it is a major holiday like Thanksgiving or Christmas or even some other special holiday or occasion, your enjoyment depends, to a large degree, on the planning. Plan menus for every meal. Make a list of the dishes you will serve. This is a fun list to make! Usually there are some traditional family favorites; write them down. Ask family members what their favorite foods are.

- **MAKE A LIST OF RECIPES.** Make a list of all the recipes you will prepare. Don't hesitate to try some new ones.

- **PRACTICE ALL NEW RECIPES AHEAD OF TIME.** If you are planning to prepare new dishes, try them ahead of time. The holiday times are usually not a good time to experiment with something new for the first time.

- **MAKE A TO-DO LIST.** The to-do list should include everything that goes with the holiday meal, such as what centerpiece you will place on the table and even what dishes, silverware, tablecloth, and napkins you will use.

- **PREPARE A SHOPPING LIST.** Now that you have menus and recipes, make out your shopping list. Check all the recipes to be sure you have all the necessary ingredients. This kind of preparation will reduce your stress levels. (A *Natural Lifestyle Cooking* **grocery list for the recipes in the cookbook is included in the workbook appendix on pages 146, 147.**)

- **HAVE A COOKING PLAN.** Look at your menus carefully. Put together a cooking plan. Are there some items that can be prepared ahead of time and still retain the nutritional value? What items can be prepared ahead without a loss of quality and taste? Make those recipes ahead. Choose recipes that are healthful for your family. Cooking ahead is a stress reliever. Of course, you can always prepare the dinner rolls and various kinds of bread ahead and freeze them. Many desserts can also be made ahead as they will keep fresh for quite a while. Plan adequate time to prepare your meal. Rushing around at the last minute will only add stress for you and your guests. When you have prepared well, things go smoothly.

- **CONSIDER HAVING PLENTY OF FRESH FRUITS AND VEGETABLES.** Remember, you can always buy pre-cut fruits and vegetables if you don't have time to prepare them. Having lots of fresh fruits and vegetables always adds to the color of the occasion and the health of your family.

- **LET FAMILY MEMBERS PARTICIPATE.** Sometimes we get the idea that if family and friends come to our home, we have to do all the preparations. Preparing holiday meals together adds to the enjoyment of the meal. Think of how this one thing alone relieves stress. Let your family and friends help in the cleanup as well. Do you remember that old saying, "Many hands make light work"? Well, have everyone work together. You will see how much fun it is as well. Family members and friends will actually enjoy contributing to the holiday meals.

- **MAKE HOLIDAY MEALS FUN.** When your family and friends arrive at your home, be sure to make it a pleasurable event. **Relax and enjoy your loved ones.** You are **making memories.** Don't spend all day cooking and cleaning up and miss the joy of the day.

Special Occasions

BIRTHDAYS

Birthdays are a special time to affirm those we care about. **They are memorable experiences.** Think about the birthdays you have experienced. Can you remember a special birthday card, gift, or celebration? Maybe you chose the menu and your favorite dessert. Didn't it make you feel special? But have you ever noticed that your children are often hyperactive on their birthdays? One reason might be the sugar-laden desserts. The question is, How can **birthday celebrations be both happy occasions and healthy ones?** Birthdays are more than invitations, decorations, and party games. One major feature is the birthday meal and dessert. A cake loaded with sugar is not the healthiest for children. Since most children grow up expecting a sugar-laden cake with thick frosting, any healthy alternative must look and taste really good. We are certainly not recommending that birthday cakes be omitted. Instead, we are recommending that you seek out healthy alternatives. This is exactly what these classes, the *Natural Lifestyle Cooking* cookbook, and this workbook are all about. In the cookbook, we have some healthy cakes, ice cream, and other suggestions. Consider the delicious **CAROB CAKE** on page 155, in the *Natural Lifestyle Cooking* cookbook.

CAROB CAKE is one of our birthday party favorites.

STRAWBERRY SHORTCAKE is another tasty birthday treat. The fresh strawberries give added nutrition. But remember, these healthful desserts are desserts. They are not the major source of our nutrients. We don't eat them every day. But we can eat them with joy, knowing that they are far better than the commercially made desserts filled with sugar, dairy products, and chemical additives. So **plan ahead, prepare healthful desserts,** and **enjoy your birthday celebrations.** A recipe for STRAWBERRY SHORTCAKE can be found in the dessert section of the workbook on page 139.

5. WHAT ARE THE ADVANTAGES OF HOMEMADE ICE CREAM OVER TRADITIONAL STORE-BOUGHT ICE CREAMS?

A. _____

B. _____

C. _____

D. _____

Homemade ice cream is delicious and nutritious. **Eliminating the dairy products and reducing the fat and cholesterol is a large benefit.** Tasty, healthy ice cream with less sugar also cuts down on the destruction of the white blood cells, which weaken the immune system. Damaged immune systems make us more prone to infection. Making homemade ice cream can be a real family affair and fun to make.

Try the nutritious **BANANA SPLITS** loaded with fresh fruit.

How about having some delicious, nutritious homemade soy ice cream? Many children would even enjoy the fruit skewers at their birthday parties.

WEDDINGS • SHOWERS • PARTIES

Giving a **bridal shower** for the bride-to-be or a **baby shower** for the new mom is a happy occasion and lots of fun. Although my husband and I have been married for more than forty-five years, I still remember the thrill of the wedding shower that my friends gave me in Hartford, Connecticut. It is a cherished memory. Through the years I have had the privilege of having many wedding and baby showers for others in my home. Every time you host a bridal or baby shower, it is an opportunity to **make positive memories** for someone. All the planning and effort you put into it is more than worthwhile. In addition to the decorations, gifts, and games, you need to think about the food that you will be serving. Let's look at a few ideas:

6. **LIST HINTS FOR GREAT SHOWERS.**

    A. _____

    B. _____

    C. _____

    D. _____

When a couple becomes engaged, generally it is one of the happiest times of their lives.

Enjoy healthy eating at the wedding shower. The **POTATO SALAD** recipe is found in the *Natural Lifestyle Cooking* cookbook, page 98. You can serve tofu **"EGG SALAD"** wedding-bell sandwiches on whole-wheat and oatmeal bread for the wedding shower.

A wedding shower captures this joy. Many brides-to-be look back at their shower as one of the most memorable experiences of their lives. Baby showers also are great times of celebration. Here are some hints for planning either a wedding or baby shower. **Make both the food and environment attractive. Use decorations appropriate to the occasion.** Decorations and foods designed for the specific event bring an added flavor of specialness. Be sure to use **cheerful colors** in the decorations and the dishes you prepare. Serve **tasty, nutritious** food.

Serving delicious **ORANGE JUICE PUNCH** at any party event is always refreshing!

VALENTINE'S DAY

Valentine's Day is extremely popular in the United States, Canada, the United Kingdom, and other countries around the world. More cards are exchanged on Valentine's Day than any other day of the year except Christmas. By the eighteenth century in Great Britain, it was very common for friends to exchange small tokens of affection. Affection was also expressed in handwritten notes. By the 1900s, cards began to replace these handwritten notes. Hallmark Cards Inc. reported on March 20, 2012, that Hallmark had sold 144 million Valentine's Day cards in 2010.

Although Valentine's Day cards are one way of expressing affection, there are numerous other ways of expressing our love. Flowers and chocolates are one of the most popular, but not the only ways. There are some that are much more creative. In 1966, my boyfriend—who is now my husband—did something very unusual for me on Valentine's Day. He gave me a beautiful card and a book on how to make bread. **Can you imagine giving your girlfriend a cookbook on Valentine's Day?** This may seem a little strange and, yes, I was quite surprised myself. But that bread cookbook sure lasted a lot longer than chocolates, and it was healthier as well. I had a **permanent gift** to guide my family on their way to better health.

In 1967, when Mark and I were married, I thought it might be a good idea to use that gift and try making some homemade bread. I was not too successful in my first attempt, but I was determined to keep trying. Today, I make bread regularly for my family. Now I have written a healthy cookbook with not only bread recipes, but many delicious, nutritious plant-based recipes. Valentine's Day was certainly special for me many years ago. It started me on the road to a career of healthful cooking and teaching cooking classes. What a valuable gift! Why not explore creative ideas on Valentine's Day? Give something unique and different to the one you care about that will benefit that person's life. When our children were growing up, I determined to make sure every year on Valentine's Day they had a card and a gift from us. I still give valentines to my family. Of course, now we do something special for our grandchildren. **Make Valentine's Day special for your family as well.** You may want to give just a simple flower to someone you care about. Flowers have lots of health power.

7. WHAT IS THE HEALTH BENEFIT OF EXPRESSING LOVE AND AFFECTION BY A SIMPLE FLOWER?

The Society of American Florists worked in cooperation with a research team at Rutgers University **to evaluate the emotional impact of receiving flowers.** They studied 147 women ranging in age, educational levels, careers, and lifestyle choices. The results were remarkable. Two emotions surfaced when these women received flowers—**excitement and happiness.** The researchers concluded that flowers positively affect our moods.

"A team of researchers explored the link between flowers and life satisfaction in a 10-month study of participants' behavioral and emotional responses to receiving flowers. The results show that flowers are a natural and healthful moderator of moods.

- Flowers have an immediate impact on happiness. All study participants expressed 'true' or 'excited' smiles upon receiving flowers, demonstrating extraordinary delight and gratitude. This reaction was universal, occurring in all age groups.

- Flowers have a long-term positive effect on moods. Specifically, study participants reported feeling less depressed, anxious, and agitated after receiving flowers, and demonstrated a higher sense of enjoyment and life satisfaction.

- Flowers make intimate connections. The presence of flowers led to increased contact with family and friends.

"Common sense tells us that flowers make us happy," said Dr. Haviland-Jones. "Now, science shows that not only do flowers make us happier than we know, they have strong positive effects on our emotional well being."[14]

If you want to bring excitement and happiness to someone you love, **send flowers this Valentine's Day.** Just a simple rose can make a difference.

8. **WHO RECEIVES THE BENEFIT OF ACTS OF KINDNESS?**

    A. _____

    B. _____

Expressing love through random acts of kindness makes a dramatic difference in the life of the individual expressing love and the one receiving it. Dr. James Lynch, a specialist in psychosomatic medicine at the University of Maryland's School of Medicine, makes this observation, "The more connected you are to life, the healthier you are. Love your neighbor as yourself is not just a moral mandate. It is a physiological mandate."[15] In other words, love makes a difference in your physiology, your health. Loving actions stimulate the brain to release positive chemical endorphins, which counteract the negative effects of stress. The bottom line is simply this—love heals. In general, love helps promote better health and longevity. Your health will improve as you bless others with acts of love and kindness. You can actually live longer by loving more.

PICNICS

9. **LIST THE BENEFITS OF FAMILY PICNICS AND EATING OUTSIDE.**

    A. _____

    B. _____

    C. _____

Going on a picnic with family and friends is always a special occasion, and the food always taste so good outside.

The Fourth of July is an American national holiday. It is often a time when families go on picnics. Picnics are enjoyable times. Food seems to taste even better in the fresh air, whether we are at a park, the beach, the mountains, or just in our own backyards. On sunny days, plan to eat outside as much as possible; you will enjoy your food more, and everyone will be more relaxed. If you use paper plates and plastic utensils, there will be less to clean up. As an added benefit of being outside, you will get beneficial amounts of **vitamin D.** Studies indicate the more relaxed we are when we eat, the more benefits we receive from our food. There is some indication that high stress levels significantly affect the digestive process. A picnic in a quiet country setting or something as simple as eating out on your back patio in a relaxed fashion can contribute to your overall health and well-being. Have you ever noticed how much better sweet corn and watermelon taste on a picnic? What about vegetarian hot dogs or home-baked beans? Picnic meals in the fresh air and sunshine, combined with games and activities with your family, will contribute to your overall well-being.

WEEKLY SPECIAL OCCASION

God gave Israel health laws that would build their health, reduce their disease, and increase their life span. Even today, although it is thirty-five hundred years since these health principles were given to Moses, the Jews have lower rates of heart disease than the general population. Just as God promised Israel good health as they followed the Creator's laws, He promises us health and longevity as we incorporate these principles into our lives.

In the Old Testament the **health of the Israelites stands out in stark contrast to that of the Egyptians.** "If you diligently heed the voice of the LORD your God and do what is right in His sight, give ear to His commandments and keep all His statutes, I will put none of the diseases on you which I have brought on the Egyptians, for I am the LORD who heals you" (Exodus 15:26). Throughout the Exodus, God was faithful to His people Israel. "There was none feeble among His tribes" (Psalm 105:37). These Bible passages, of course, are not promises that we will never get sick. We live in a world polluted by sin, and sickness and disease are all around us.

Studies done on Egyptian mummies confirm the truthfulness of God's word. Dr. Rosalie David of Manchester University in Manchester, England, has done extensive autopsies on Egyptian mummies and found, for example, that it is very likely that Ramses II of Egypt died of a massive heart attack. Heart disease, arthritis, obesity, high blood pressure, rheumatism, and sexually transmitted diseases were prevalent among the Egyptians.[16]

Recently, CT scans have been used to unveil the diseases of ancient Egyptians. "We like to say that we found the serial killer that stalked mankind for 4,000 years," said Dr. Randall Thompson, attending cardiologist at St. Luke's Mid America Heart Institute and lead author of a new study on the diseases of Egyptian mummies. In this study, scientists CT scanned 137 mummies and found that one-third had definite or probable atherosclerosis.[17]

10. WHAT HEALTH PRINCIPLES OF THE ANCIENT ISRAELITES CAN BENEFIT OUR LIVES TODAY?

A. _____

B. _____

C. _____

The ancient Israelites **refrained from the eating of pork and all fats** in their foods. Twenty-first-century science has confirmed the validity of a low-fat diet. The Israelites **practiced strict principles of hygiene** and the isolation of those afflicted with contagious diseases. Another of the **principles of health and longevity of the Israelites was the Sabbath.** This was a **weekly special occasion** to meet with God. Each Sabbath the Israelites entered into a covenant relationship with their Creator. Exodus 16 records the miracle of manna falling from heaven. Manna represents heaven's diet and God's provision to keep Israel healthy. "Six days you shall gather it, but on the seventh day, the Sabbath, there will be none" (Exodus 16:26). The **Israelites had their Sabbath meals prepared ahead of time** so the Sabbath could be dedicated to the worship of their God.

For the **ancient Israelites, each week provided a special occasion to celebrate.** The seventh-day Sabbath was a great day of rejoicing. Families gathered for a **special meal on Friday nights** and also at midday on Sabbath. They shared the joys of their week. They drew closer as families. On Fridays, the women spent a good portion of the day preparing delicious, healthful meals for the Sabbath. Not surprisingly, our Jewish friends have had above-average health for centuries. I have included some of **our favorite plant-based Israeli and Middle Eastern dishes** in this lesson. They are some of our favorites, and we know you will enjoy them too.

FAVORITE MIDDLE EASTERN FOODS

In the early days of the state of Israel, residents of a *kibbutz* would begin their work early in the morning before the hot midday sun. After working for several hours, they ate a hearty breakfast. Their breakfast was largely composed of bread, olives, eggs, cheese, and raw vegetables. This meal became famous and known as the **"Israeli breakfast"** and is served today to tourists in many hotels. However, for many Israelis who live in the cities, this breakfast has become increasingly rare.

Israel does not have a universally recognized national dish because the population is made up of people from various countries. However, **falafels are one of the best known Israeli and Middle Eastern dishes.** The main ingredient in falafels is mashed chickpeas, which are very nutritious. In Israel, falafels are usually served in pita pocket bread with hummus, and at times, tomatoes, lettuce, and tahini sauce mixed in. Today, falafel sandwiches are sold on the streets by vendors throughout Israel. Falafels are one of our family favorites. I hope you enjoy them as much as we do. (FALAFEL recipe is on page 74 of the *Natural Lifestyle Cooking* cookbook.)

Nutritious favorite foods of the Middle East—**FALAFELS,** hummus with pita bread, **TABOULI,** and abundance of grapes.

Fresh-squeezed orange juice and **ORANGE WEDGES** are a favorite in the Middle East.

Orange Wedges

CUT oranges in half lengthwise. **CUT** into six wedges. **ARRANGE** on a plate and **SERVE.**

Fresh fruit is often served as dessert along with Middle Eastern pastries such as baklava and macaroons. Other **typical plant-based foods are flat bread, lentils, hummus with pita bread, Israeli salad, cooked sweet carrots and other cooked vegetables, raw vegetables, fresh fruits, and nuts.**

A wonderful **Jewish expression**—*Shabbat Shalom*—speaks of a **peaceful heart,** a **restful spirit,** and a **healthy body.** The expression can be literally translated **"may the peace, rest, joy, and health of the Sabbath surround you and fill your life."** It is our prayer that as you make positive steps toward better health, your life will be filled with peace, rest, and joy as well.

HOSPITALITY

What is hospitality? *Hospitality* might be defined as "a gracious attitude toward others." It is a warm, friendly, welcoming, generous, kind attitude. Hospitality can be practiced at all times and all places. The church is an excellent place to exhibit a hospitable spirit. It is a wonderful place to entertain family, friends, neighbors, and even strangers. But hospitality is typically thought of as cordially welcoming people into our homes. The home should be a haven of rest and relaxation. It is also a wonderful place for others to feel at home and enjoy the atmosphere. We desire our personal home to always be a warm, friendly, and inviting place for family and friends.

Our personal home has always been and will be **a place for our children and grandchildren** to call home. We try to provide an atmosphere that is relaxing and enjoyable for them. Besides for our family, our home has also been **a place where our friends come to enjoy fellowship** as well. In fact, through the years we have had many people besides our family members live in our home.

There are **many benefits to being hospitable,** including growing closer family ties, deepening existing friendships, and meeting great new people. Of course, this is not the main reason for our hospitality. We are hospitable because we genuinely care about others. And, most of all, we should cultivate an attitude of enjoying hospitality. "Be hospitable to one another without grumbling" (1 Peter 4:9).

Practicing hospitality can prove to be a real blessing. Many times guests will offer to bring something to contribute to the meal. If they do, accept. It will be a help to you, and they will feel they are making a contribution to the meal. In the process of being more hospitable, you will strengthen family ties, make new friends, and enjoy life more. After all, **it is positive, healthy relationships that bring life's greatest joy.**

TIPS FOR HOSPITALITY IN THE HOME

- **CULTIVATE** the spirit of hospitality. Remember, there is a difference between entertainment and hospitality. Entertaining often means everything has to be perfect before you invite guests to come to your home. Hospitality means even if everything is not perfect, you still can have great fellowship.

- **INVITE** people to your home. Be willing to invite friends, people in the neighborhood, and people from church to your home for dinner. Invite the widows, singles, or needy to your home. Remember the biblical admonition, "Do not forget to entertain strangers, for by so doing some have unwittingly entertained angels" (Hebrews 13:2). As you invite people to your home, you may be blessed beyond what you can imagine.

- **CREATE** a warm, friendly, enjoyable atmosphere. When our married children and grandchildren visit us, we like to prepare their rooms ahead of time with something special just for them. It might be a toy for the grandkids or some special treat. You can do the same for overnight guests too.

- **SHARE** with family and friends places to shop, points of interest, or recreational activities in the area. If your family or guests are from out of town, keep a local travel guidebook for them to find some of their favorite places to visit.

- **PLACE** reading material in your guest rooms. It is nice to set out some good books and magazines for your guests to read. Have plenty of children's books when the grandchildren come.

- **ENSURE** that your guests have plenty of towels, washcloths, and any extra bedding, such as pillows or blankets.

- **PROVIDE** plenty of water. They will appreciate either bottled water or a pitcher with glasses in the bedroom or bathroom. I know this is a very important item for both my husband and me as we travel. Since we drink at least two glasses of water in the morning when we wake up, we look for those bottles of water in our room.

- **STOCK** a basket of essentials in your guest bathroom. Family or guests will appreciate it if they forgot their shampoo, toothbrush, or toothpaste!

- **PREPARE** those extra special touches to help your family and guests feel welcome and at home. You may want to place a scented candle in their room or make sure your guests have an alarm clock, especially if they have an early morning appointment.

- **GIVE** your family and guests plenty of privacy and space.

- **ALLOW** your guests to help you. When guests ask, "Is there something I can help you with?" Say, "Yes," because you probably really do need the help, and most people will feel more comfortable when they are involved. You will find that having guests in your home is a pleasure when everyone works together.

As you **incorporate the principles of** *Natural Lifestyle Cooking* **and** *WELLNESS* **included in this workbook,** your **health will improve,** and you will have a **greater sense of well-being.** You will discover that a plant-based nutritious diet is tasty and enjoyable. My wish for you is that you will eat well, so that you will be well, stay well, prosper, and be in health.

ANSWERS TO CLASS 6

1. 1. Eat moderately.
    2. Make wise choices.
    3. Limit desserts.
    4. Get some exercise.
    5. Enjoy relationships.
    6. Surprise someone with kindness.
    7. Be thankful.

2. The immune system is a system of biological structures and processes within an organism that protects against disease.

3. Follow good-health guidelines.

4. Almonds, Brazil nuts, pecans, and walnuts (without added salt or oil)

5. A. No dairy—reducing the fat content
    B. No eggs—eliminating the highest source of cholesterol
    C. No preservatives
    D. Less sugar, no white sugar

6. A. Attractive and appropriate to the occasion
    B. Colorful
    C. Nutritious
    D. Tasty

7. Excitement and happiness

8. A. One expressing love
    B. One receiving love

9. A. Fresh air—food is more appetizing
    B. Sunshine—vitamin D
    C. Relaxation—Reduced stress

10. A. Reduced dietary fat
    B. Temperate lifestyle
    C. Sabbath rest

ENDNOTES

1. "In Praise of Gratitude," accessed May 23, 2013, http://www.health.harvard.edu/newsletters/Harvard_Mental_Health_Letter/2011/November/in-praise-of-gratitude.

2. Elizabeth Heubeck, "Boost Your Health With a Dose of Gratitude," accessed April 22, 2013, http://women.webmd.com/features/gratitude-health-boost.

3. "Power of a Super Attitude," USA Today, October 12, 2004.

4. Mike Gilbert, "An Attitude of Gratitude," SermonCentral, accessed July 24, 2013, http://www.sermoncentral.com/sermons/an-attitude-of-gratitude-mike-gilbert-sermon-on-joy-113888.asp?page=4.

5. "How to Boost Your Immune System: What Can You Do?" accessed May 7, 2013, http://www.health.harvard.edu/flu-resource-center/how-to-boost-your-immune-system.htm.

6. Ibid.

7. Ellen G. White, The Ministry of Healing (Mountain View, Calif.: Pacific Press®, 1942), 127.

8. "Eating Nuts Promotes Cardiovacascular Health," accessed May 6, 2013, http://www.health.harvard.edu/press_releases/benefits_eating_nuts.

9. Accessed April 23, 2013, http://nutritiondata.self.com/facts/nut-and-seed-products/3085/2.

10. "They're Good for Us, but Which Nut Is the Best?" accessed April 23, 2013, http://www.health.harvard.edu/fhg/updates/update1004d.shtml.

11. Accessed April 23, 2013, http://nutritiondata.self.com/facts/nut-and-seed-products/3129/2.

12. Accessed April 23, 2013, http://nutritiondata.self.com/facts/nut-and-seed-products/3138/2.

13. J. Sabaté, American Journal of Clinical Nutrition (September 1999): 70, abstract in http://www.ncbi.nlm.nih.gov/pubmed/10479222, accessed May 23, 2013.

14. "Rutgers: Flowers Improve Emotional Health," accessed March 19, 2013, http://www.flowerpossibilities.com/2010/08/emotional-impact-of-flowers-study.

15. "The Healing Power of Love," accessed March 19, 2013, http://www.transformationnow.net/2010/06/the-healing-power-of-love.

16. Hannah Devlin, "Scans of Egyptian Mummies Reveal Heart Disease Is Not Just a Modern Curse," Australian Times, accessed May 7, 2013, http://www.theAustralian.com.au/news/health-science/scans-of-egyptian-mummies-reveal-heart-disease-is-not-just-a-modern-curse/story-e6frg8y6.

17. "Lessons About Disease . . . From Mummies," accessed May 7, 2013, http://thechart.blogs.cnn.com/2013/03/10/lessons-about-disease-from-mummies.

Class 7

Simple, Healthful Desserts

Desserts · Diabetes

A group of dietitians published a pamphlet on the **harmful effects of excessive sugar consumption.** The pamphlet begins with this fascinating sentence: "Judging by the size of America's sugar bowl, it really ought to be a sweet world."[1] Someone has said, "Every day in America is sweeter than the day before," and it certainly is!

According to a survey by the United States Department of Agriculture, Americans eat approximately 3,500,000 pounds of candy each year. That's about sixteen pounds for every man, woman, and child in the country. This is only the beginning of the story. America's sweet tooth seems to get bigger each year. Our craving for sweets seems more intense each passing decade. The average American consumes a whopping amount of sugar yearly. The increase in sugar consumption over the last two hundred years has been remarkable.[2]

1. WHAT IS THE INCREASE OF SUGAR CONSUMPTION PER DAY FOR THE AVERAGE AMERICAN OVER APPROXIMATELY TWO HUNDRED YEARS?

1822 _____ TEASPOONS PER DAY

1890 _____ TEASPOONS PER DAY

1905 _____ TEASPOONS PER DAY

The increase in sugar consumption from the early eighteen hundreds until now has been remarkable. This increase has paralleled a rise in degenerative lifestyle diseases. In 1822, Americans consumed 2 teaspoons of sugar per day. In 1890, 10 teaspoons a day were consumed. By 1905, the number of teaspoons doubled. Americans were now eating 20 teaspoons of sugar daily. By 2001, it was 22. And today the number of teaspoons consumed daily is an amazing 27.5.[3]

From 2001 to 2013, the average American ate an average of 22 teaspoons of sugar each day. Teens eat on the average 32 teaspoons per day.[4]

Sugar consumption went up consistently from 1822 to 2000. In 1970, the average American was eating 70 pounds of sugar per year. By 2000, it was a whopping 90 pounds per year, and today it is at least 120 pounds a year, though some estimates put the figure as high as 156 pounds a year for each American.[5]

This is an alarming amount! **Nutritional research** continues to produce **evidence that the high-sugar content in the American diet is causing an alarming increase in degenerative diseases.**

"Sugar provides calories and no other nutrients."[6] The quick absorption of sucrose, the form of sugar familiar as table sugar, is the reason why it seems to give us a quick energy lift or pickup. There are **several problems,** however, with this quick absorption of sucrose. Because carbohydrates require a number of B vitamins for the body to process them, and sugar itself contains no B vitamins, the body must draw on its reserves, creating the possibility of a **vitamin B deficiency.** High-sugar intake has also been associated with

- **TYPE 2 DIABETES**
- **OBESITY**
- **MALNUTRITION (EMPTY CALORIES)**
- **WEAKENED IMMUNE SYSTEM**
- **INCREASED TOOTH DECAY**
- **HEART DISEASE**
- **HYPOGLYCEMIA: LOW BLOOD SUGAR**
- **INFECTION: SUSCEPTIBILITY TO DISEASE**
- **IRRITABILITY**

Let's examine these health-destroying effects of excessive sugar more closely.

HEALTH HAZARDS OF A HIGH-SUGAR DIET

2. WHAT ARE THE TWO MOST CRITICAL HEALTH ISSUES IN THE UNITED STATES TODAY RELATED TO EXCESSIVE SUGAR?

A. _____

B. _____

"Diabetes and obesity are two of the most critical health issues in the United States today, with millions of dollars poured into research every year to further uncover the sources of this epidemic in order to cure the disease. Researchers at the Yale School of Medicine, working with Dr. Varman Samuel, Assistant Professor of Endocrinology, have recently uncovered a feed-forward mechanism whereby excess sugar consumption may lead to increased fat production in the liver and the ensuing development of diabetes."[7]

OBESITY

3. WHAT ARE THE CURRENT STATISTICS ON THOSE WHO ARE CONSIDERED OVERWEIGHT OR OBESE IN THE UNITED STATES?

"More Americans are becoming overweight or obese, exercising less, and eating unhealthy foods. That's the finding of the latest Gallup-Healthways Well-Being Index, which shows that 63.1% of adults in the U.S. were either overweight or obese in 2009."[8]

Because **obesity contributes to heart disease, a diet high in sugar and fat is certainly a major culprit.** Although there are many risk factors contributing to coronary artery disease, excessive sugar consumption is certainly one of them.

4. WHAT PERCENTAGE OF CHILDREN AND ADOLESCENTS AGES TWO TO NINETEEN IN THE UNITED STATES ARE OVERWEIGHT OR OBESE?

Obesity is becoming an increasing problem among young people ages two to nineteen. Recent statistics indicate that approximately 32 percent are overweight or obese.[9]

Childhood obesity has become a very serious medical issue. It occurs when children are above the normal weight for their age. Health problems such as diabetes and high cholesterol are recently beginning to occur at a very young age. Obesity often leads children to have **low self-esteem** and **depression.** One of the best ways to reduce the plague of childhood obesity is to **improve the lifestyle habits of the entire family,** particularly by diet and exercise. Be diligent about making sure your children eat healthfully and get adequate exercise.

Average Americans get 20 percent of their calories from the 156 pounds of sugar they eat each year. Many people find it easier to overeat refined concentrated foods. Sugar calories not used by the body are **stored as fat.** A refined sugary diet is a major factor in the problem of obesity. The Harvard School of Public Health Newsletter made the following observation:

"What's become the typical Western diet—frequent, large meals high in refined grains, red meat, unhealthy fats, and sugary drinks—plays one of the largest roles in obesity. Foods that are lacking in the Western diet—whole grains, vegetables, fruits, and nuts—seem to help with weight control, and also help prevent chronic disease."[10]

The prevalence of fast foods and the so-called empty calorie junk foods make it very difficult for many people to make healthy choices to maintain their ideal weight and reduce chronic diseases. An informed, disciplined choice to eat a diet high in plant-based foods will result in both a better quality of life and longer life.

DIABETES

The high intake of sugar is a major factor in obesity. A Harvard School of Public Health report revealed that "the condition most strongly influenced by body weight is type 2 diabetes. In the Nurses' Health Study, which followed 114,000 middle-age women for 14 years, the risk of developing diabetes was 93 times higher among women who had a body mass index (BMI) of 35 or higher at the start of the study, compared with women with BMIs lower than 22. Weight gain during adulthood also increased diabetes risk, even among women with BMIs in the healthy range." The Health Professionals Follow-Up Study found a similar association in men.[11]

Cutting out sugar-laden soft drinks may be a good way to control some of the challenges of obesity and type 2 diabetes. An article titled "Sugar Sweetened Soft Drinks, Obesity and Type 2 Diabetes" reported that "sugar-sweetened soft drinks contribute 7.1 percent of total energy intake and represent the largest single food source of calories in the US diet. Coincidentally or not, the rise of obesity and type 2 diabetes in the United States parallels the increase in sugar-sweetened soft drink consumption. Several studies have found an association between sugar-sweetened beverages and incidence of obesity in children. In one study, the odds ratio of becoming obese increased 1.6 times for each additional sugar-sweetened drink consumed every day. Increased diet soda consumption was negatively associated with childhood obesity."[12]

Diabetes is usually a chronic (long-term) disease in which the blood contains high levels of sugar. It is a group of metabolic diseases in which the person has high blood glucose (blood sugar) either because insulin production is inadequate or because the body's cells do not respond properly to insulin, or both.

5. **LIST THE THREE MOST COMMON TYPES OF DIABETES.**

A. _____

B. _____

C. _____

Let's look at some critical points on each type of diabetes.

TYPE 1 DIABETES

- The body does not produce insulin.
- The individual is insulin dependent.
- This is an early onset diabetes or juvenile diabetes.
- It usually develops before a person's fortieth birthday.
- Approximately 10 percent of all diabetes cases are type 1.
- The individual needs to take insulin injections for the rest of his or her life.

TYPE 2 DIABETES

- The body does not produce enough insulin for proper function, or the cells in the body do not react to insulin.

- Approximately 90 percent of all cases of diabetes worldwide are of this type.

- Some people may be able to control their type 2 diabetes symptoms by losing weight, following a healthy diet, getting plenty of exercise, and monitoring their blood glucose levels.

- Typically this is a progressive disease.

- Overweight and obese people have a much higher risk of developing type 2 diabetes compared to those who maintain a healthy weight.

GESTATIONAL DIABETES

- This type of diabetes affects only females during pregnancy.

- The body is unable to produce enough insulin to transport all the glucose into their cells, resulting in rising levels of glucose.[13]

MALNUTRITION—EMPTY CALORIES

Refined sugar has no nutritional value. It supplies us with quick energy, but nothing else. It lacks the fiber, vitamins, minerals, and enzymes that create a synergistic effect for normal absorption, assimilation, and digestion. The human body was designed to assimilate the nutrients from a wide variety of wholesome foods. It was **not designed for artificially refined junk foods that are high in fat** and **sugar.** One of the reasons scores of children, youth, and adults are so often hungry and constantly eating without being satisfied is from what some nutritionists call **"hidden hunger"**—the body's craving for wholesome foods.

The following statement issued by UNICEF in 2004 points to **a global** public health issue that **prevents a third of the world's children from reaching their intellectual and physical potential.** "Vitamin and mineral deficiency is the source of the most massive 'hidden hunger' and malnutrition in the world today. The 'hidden hunger' due to micronutrient deficiency does not produce hunger as we know it. You might not feel it in the belly, but it strikes at the core of your health and vitality. It remains widespread, posing devastating threats to health, education, economic growth and to human dignity in developing countries."[14]

Our sugar and fat consumption is far too high. Dr. Roger J. Williams, a biochemist who spent thirty years in research on the nutrition of a single cell, observes: "Malnutrition—unbalanced or inadequate nutrition—at the cellular level should be thought of as a major cause of human disease. This seems crystal clear to me."[15]

6. WHAT IS MALNUTRITION?

Malnutrition is a broad term that can mean both undernutrition and overnutrition. **Undernutrition** occurs when a person is malnourished from **inadequate calories and nutrients** for growth and maintenance. **Malnutrition occurs** whenever the cells are deprived of essential vitamins, minerals, carbohydrates, and proteins they need to maintain healthy tissues and organ function. **This type of malnutrition** can occur when a person eats **empty calories.** According to the United Nation's Standing Committee on Nutrition, malnutrition is the world's largest contributor to disease.

7. **WHAT ARE TWO TYPES OF MALNUTRITION?**

   A. _____

   B. _____

The **first** and most important is **protein-energy malnutrition.** This occurs when there is a **lack of enough protein-energy producing food,** which is measured in calories that all of the basic food groups provide. **This type of malnutrition is referred to when world hunger is discussed.** According to the United Nations, malnutrition is the gravest single threat to global public health. The best estimates we have is that there were 925 million malnourished people in 2010.[16]

The **second** type of malnutrition is **micronutrient malnutrition (vitamin and mineral) deficiency.** Micronutrient deficiency occurs when there is a lack in the needed amounts of vitamins and minerals. This type of deficiency is much more likely to occur on a high-fat, high-sugar diet, which leaves out the essential vitamins and minerals contained in plant-based foods. The danger is that an individual can get adequate calories, appear quite normal, but be malnourished on the cellular level.

One of the problems that we face in the United States is the prominence of fast foods. Many **fast foods are "fat" traps.** For example, chicken nuggets dipped in a mayonnaise dip (mayonnaise is basically made up of three ingredients: oil, egg yolks, and vinegar), hamburgers, bacon-and-egg sandwiches, and similar fast foods are extremely high in cholesterol. **If we eat fast foods at all, it is important for our health that we choose wisely.** Choosing vegetable submarine sandwiches, cheeseless pizza with extra tomato sauce and lots of vegetable toppings, vegetarian bean burritos, and, of course, salads are much better choices.

A survey conducted by the Agricultural Research Service and Harvard University found a link **between fast-food consumption** by children in the United States **and increased calories and poor nutrition.**

"U.S. children who ate fast food, compared with those who did not, consumed more total calories, more calories per gram of food, more total and saturated fat, more total carbohydrate, more added sugars and more sugar-sweetened beverages, but less milk, fiber, fruit and non-starchy vegetables. The study also revealed out of the two days surveyed, those children who consumed fast food on only one day showed similar nutrient shortfalls on the day they had fast food. But they did not show these shortfalls on the other day."[17]

Eating large amounts of fast foods contributes to an excessive use of sugar. **Sugar is a large contributor of empty calories.** Research has linked the overconsumption of sugar to overeating, poor memory, learning disorders, and depression. **Most people are not aware of the large amount of sugar they are eating** because it is hidden in the foods they eat. The common conception is, "Someone else must be getting my share. Certainly I am not eating that much sugar." A more careful analysis indicates that most of us are. Even some foods promoted as health foods contain large amounts of sugar.

8. WHAT ARE SOME COMMON SOURCES OF HIDDEN SUGAR?

HIDDEN SUGARS IN FOODS[18]

FOOD	AMOUNT	TEASPOONS OF SUGAR
Banana split	Medium/large	24
Brownies	3" diameter	3
Canned fruit	1 serving	3
Chewing gum	1 piece	1/2
Chocolate candy bar	1 small	6
Chocolate cake	4 oz.	10
Fruit pie	1 slice	10
Glazed donut	1	6
Ice cream	3 scoops	12
Milkshake	1 pint	15
Soft drink	12 oz.	8
Jelly	1 tsp.	3

Most of the **commercial cereals contain large amounts of sugar.** Cheerios have very minimal amounts but most cereals average from 10 to 12 grams of sugar per serving. Margo Wootan, director of Nutrition Policy for the Center for Science in the Public Interest, a food watchdog group, comments, "Since a serving size is 30 grams or less, a third of the serving is still sugar."[19] Think of it, in most cereals for children, at least a whopping 33 percent is sugar.

WEAKENED IMMUNE SYSTEM

The excessive use of refined sugar **suppresses our immune system.** Just one serving of sugar from a soft drink, candy bar, cake, cookie, ice cream, and so on, can suppress our immune system for several hours. This leaves us vulnerable to many viruses. Our **health suffers when we regularly eat excessive sugar.**

TOOTH DECAY

Sugar is easily fermented by bacteria in the mouth. Animals on an experimental high-sugar diet were observed to have blocked fluid movement in the canals of their teeth, causing rapid deterioration. During World War II, Norway had a significant reduction in its supply of sugar. This decrease in sugar supply caused a reduction in sugar consumption that continued from

1939 to 1945. During the war years, a 50 to 70 percent reduction in tooth decay was noted.[20]

"Eating patterns and food choices among children and teens are important factors that affect how quickly youngsters may develop tooth decay. The reason is a sticky film of bacteria called 'plaque' constantly forms on the teeth and gums. Each and every time bacteria come in contact with sugar or starch in the mouth, acid is produced that attacks the teeth for twenty minutes or more. This eventually can result in tooth decay."[21]

HEART DISEASE

Although many risk factors contribute to coronary artery disease, **excessive sugar consumption** has been implicated as one possible risk factor.

Dr. John Yudkin was professor of nutrition and dietetics at the University of London from 1954 to 1971. He demonstrated "that the consumption of sugar and refined sweeteners is closely associated with coronary heart disease and type 2 diabetes."[22]

Dr. John Yudkin's studies at the University of London found that **men who suffered heart attacks ate twice as much sugar than their male counterparts whose hearts were healthy.** The average American gets 20 percent of his or her calories from the 156 pounds of sugar that he or she eats every year. Investigators also discovered that fat and sugar together tend to elevate fatty substances in the blood stream much higher than either one alone.

In other words, the higher the sugar content in your diet, the more likely you are to have a coronary heart attack. Dr. Yudkin's research was published in his popular book titled *Pure, White and Deadly: How Sugar Is Killing Us and What We Can Do to Stop It.* In his ground-breaking research, Dr. Yudkin links excessive sugar to many of the chronic diseases in Western society.

HYPOGLYCEMIA: LOW BLOOD SUGAR

Many physicians are concluding that **America's excessive sugar consumption,** especially between meals, tends to cause the blood sugar levels to rapidly rise, then fall quickly below normal levels. The corresponding high of quick energy is followed by a corresponding low of **tiredness and lethargy.** This is true of all stimulants.

INFECTION: SUSCEPTIBILITY TO DISEASE

Another important factor to consider is the **relationship between sugar intake and the body's ability to fight disease.** When there is danger of infection, the white blood cells increase in number in the blood stream. These soldiers of the body destroy bacteria, the infection-causing

EFFECT OF SUGAR INTAKE ON THE ABILITY OF WHITE BLOOD CELLS (WBC) TO DESTROY BACTERIA[23]

Teaspoons of sugar eaten at one time by an average adult	Number of bacteria destroyed by each WBC in 30 minutes	Percentage decrease in ability to destroy bacteria
0	14	0 percent
6	10	25 percent
12	5.5	60 percent
18	1	85 percent
24	1	92 percent

agent. But when the blood sugar level goes up, they become sluggish and cannot destroy as many bacteria. Studies done by Loma Linda University indicate there is a significant temporary decrease in the ability of certain white blood cells, the phagocytes, to destroy bacteria after a person eats a large amount of sugar at one time. Normal levels of white blood cell activity do not return until five to six hours later.

IRRITABILITY

"Excessive sugar and the lack of vitamin B complex and certain minerals result in the incomplete metabolism of sugar to carbon dioxide and cause pyruvic acid build up with neutralization of vitamin B, resulting in irritability."[24]

Ellen White, a nineteenth-century health promoter, said, "Sugar is not good for the stomach. It causes fermentation, and this clouds the brain and brings peevishness into the disposition. . . .

"Sugar clogs the system. It hinders the working of the living machine."[25]

Limiting the amount of sugar we eat will give us clear thoughts, a better disposition, and a healthier body. So, must we give up all desserts? No! Simply choose wisely. Choose healthful desserts and limit the amount you eat. After all, they are still desserts. My *Natural Lifestyle Cooking* cookbook includes some good dessert choices.

RECIPES FOR SIMPLE, HEALTHFUL DESSERTS

Banana-Strawberry Ice Cream

Frozen bananas
Frozen strawberries
Chopped walnuts
Melted Chatfield's carob chips

PUT as many frozen bananas and strawberries that you would like to feed your guests through a commercial juicer. **DRIBBLE** the carob sauce on top of the bananas, and **SPRINKLE** with walnuts.

BANANA-STRAWBERRY ICE CREAM is an all-natural dish with frozen bananas and frozen strawberries pressed through a Champion® juicer. This ice-cream fruit dish is even more delicious when you sprinkle crushed walnuts and melted carob chips on top. It is great for a simple, healthful dessert.

FRESH FRUIT: Fresh fruit is the dessert prepared especially for us by our loving Creator. It is delicious, colorful, and health promoting. Take advantage of a slice of watermelon in season. It is appetizing, very refreshing, and low in calories. A melon fruit plate is always attractive and appealing. Using fresh fruit for dessert is also time-saving and provides wonderful taste and quality nutrition.

You can serve high-antioxidant foods on fruit skewers for a simple, healthful dessert or even at special celebration events.

Strawberry Shortcake

SHORTCAKE:

¼ c. Earth Balance® margarine spread

¼ c. brown sugar

1 t. egg replacer/1 T. water

1 ½ c. soymilk

½ c. soy creamer

2 c. unbleached enriched flour

1 T. wheat germ

2 t. Rumford® baking powder

6 c. fresh strawberries, sliced

2 T. honey

Whipped soy cream

CREAM Earth Balance® margarine spread and brown sugar together. **ADD** the egg replacer. **ADD** soymilk and soy creamer. **MIX** in flour, wheat germ, and baking powder. **POUR** into oiled 8 x 1 ½ inch round baking dish. **BAKE** at 425°F for 18 to 20 minutes. **COOL** in pan. **CUT** shortcake piece in two layers or leave the shortcake piece whole. **ADD** honey to the strawberries. **PLACE** strawberries over shortcake. **ADD** whipped soy cream.

TIPS FOR CONTROLLING SUGAR INTAKE

- **READ LABELS.** It is imperative that all ingredients be listed with the greatest amounts listed first. Avoid foods with high sugar content.

- **AVOID USING SUGAR AT THE TABLE.** Avoid adding extra sugar to hot drinks, cereals, and other foods.

- **CHOOSE HEALTHIER RECIPES.** Choose recipes with little or no sugar, or use natural sugars, such as dates or other dried fruit.

- **AVOID SUGAR-COATED COMMERCIAL CEREALS.** Most cereals on the market have high sugar contents. Read labels. If sugar is near the top of the ingredient list, beware.

- **EAT DESSERTS ONLY OCCASIONALLY.** Discipline yourself to eat desserts only once or twice a week and on holidays and special occasions such as birthdays.

- **ELIMINATE SOFT DRINKS.** Completely eliminate soft drinks because they contain large amounts of sugar and chemicals.

- **USE 100 PERCENT FRUIT JUICES.** Use 100 percent fruit juices rather than fruit drinks with added refined sugar.

- **REPLACE REFINED SUGAR WITH NATURAL SUGARS.** Replace refined sugar with natural sugars such as honey, dates, etc.

- **CHOOSE FRUIT DESSERTS.** Fresh fruit is high in antioxidants. It is naturally sweet and loaded with vitamins and minerals.

- **EXPERIMENT WITH CUTTING THE SUGAR CONTENT.** Remember, you can cut the sugar content in half in many recipes.

- **CHOOSE SMALLER PORTIONS.** When you do have desserts, discipline yourself to choose smaller portions.

- **SET OUT DESSERTS IN PLAIN SIGHT.** Seeing the desserts that are being served enables you to plan ahead how much you are going to eat. You will be able to save room for dessert.

Our bodies were designed to assimilate the nutrients from a wide variety of wholesome foods—fruits, vegetables, grains, and nuts. It was **not designed for junk foods** high in fat and sugar and refined artificially. One of the reasons scores of children, youth, and adults are hungry so often and constantly eating without being satisfied is because of **hidden hunger. Their bodies crave wholesome foods.** As you feed your family wholesome, nutritious meals, they will be really satisfied. The constant nibbling to fill that "empty hole" will be replaced with a sense of satisfied fullness. Your family will anticipate meals, enjoy them, and reap the benefits of good health.

The ancient Scriptures declare, **"Beloved, I pray that you may prosper in all things and be in health, just as your soul prospers" (3 John 2).** Humans are physical, mental, and spiritual beings. Health consists of physical well-being, mental alertness, and spiritual harmony or peace.

My wish for you is a life of abundant physical health filled with zest, vitality, and energy, a life of mental joy, inner peace, and happy relationships with those around you, and spiritual commitment to the God who created you and longs to be your best Friend.

ANSWERS TO CLASS 7

1. 2, 10, 20

2. A. Obesity
   B. Diabetes

3. About 63 percent are either overweight or obese.

4. Approximately 32 percent

5. A. Type 1 diabetes
   B. Type 2 diabetes
   C. Gestational diabetes

6. Malnutrition develops when the body does not receive adequate vitamins, minerals, and other nutrients.

7. A. Protein-energy malnutrition
   B. Micronutrient malnutrition—vitamin and mineral deficiency

8. See chart on page 136.

ENDNOTES

1. "Sugar: The Unsweetened Truth," accessed January 24, 2013, http://nurturing-naturally.com/2010/09/29/sugar-the-unsweetened-truth.
2. Nancy Schmieder, "Too Much Sugar," accessed January 24, 2013, http://www.beyondthebend.com/health/toomuchsugar.htm.
3. Ethel R. Nelson, *375 Meatless Recipes* (Leominister, Mass.: Eusey Press, 1974), 135.
4. Accessed January 24, 2013, http://wiki.answers.com/Q/How_many_teaspoons_of_sugar_does_the_average_American_eat_per_day.
5. John Casey, "The Hidden Ingredient That Can Sabotage Your Diet," accessed July 29, 2013, http://www.medicinenet.com/script/main/art.asp?articlekey=56589.
6. "Sugar," Seventh-day Adventist Dietetic Association, 2.
7. Jenny Mei, "Research Links Sugar Consumption, Fat Production, and Diabetes," accessed January 27, 2013, http://www.yalescientific.org/2011/04/research-links-sugar-consumption-fat-production-and-diabetes.
8. Bill Hendrick, "Percentage of Overweight, Obese Americans Swells," WebMD, accessed June 12, 2013, http://www.webmd.com/diet/news/20100210/percentage-of-overweight-obese-americans-swells.
9. "Overweight and Obesity Statistics," Weight-control Information Network, accessed June 12, 2013, http://win.niddk.nih.gov/statistics.
10. "Obesity Causes," accessed May 8, 2013, http://www.hsph.harvard.edu/obesity-prevention-source/obesity-causes.
11. "Health Risks," accessed January 24, 2013, http://www.hsph.harvard.edu/obesity-prevention-source/obesity-consequences/health-effects.
12. Caroline M. Apovian, "Sugar-Sweetened Soft Drinks, Obesity, and Type 2 Diabetes," accessed May 23, 2013, http://nepc.colorado.edu/files/CERU-0410-237-OWI.pdf.
13. Nicky Pilkington, "The Different Types of Diabetes," accessed May 8, 2013, http://www.healthguidance.org/entry/4942/1/The-Different-Types-of-Diabetes.html.
14. "The Hidden Hunger of the Vitamin and Mineral Deficient Child," accessed January 24, 2013, http://www.unicef.org/nutrition/index_hidden_hunger.html.
15. Roger J. Williams, *Nutrition Against Disease* (New York: Bantam Books, 1973), 34.
16. "2012 World Hunger and Poverty Facts and Statistics," accessed May 28, 2013, http://www.worldhunger.org/articles/Learn/world%20hunger%20facts%202002.htm.
17. Rosalie Marion Bliss, "Survey Links Fast Food, Poor Nutrition Among U.S. Children," accessed January 27, 2013, http://www.ars.usda.gov/is/pr/2004/040105.htm.

18.   Nelson, *375 Meatless Recipes,* 135.

19.   Julie Jargon, "Success Is Only So Sweet in Remaking Cereals," *Wall Street Journal,* October 11, 2011.

20.   "Diet and Tooth Decay," accessed January 27, 2013, www.ada.org/sections/scienceandresearch/pdfs/patient_13.pdf.

21.   Ibid.

22.   "Is Science on Toxicity of Sugar New? Not Exactly," accessed March 19, 2013, http://carbsyndrome.com/is-science-on -toxicity-of-sugar-new-not-exactly.

23.   Albert Sanchez et al., "Role of Sugars in Human Neutrophilic Phagocytosis," *American Journal of Clinical Nutrition* 26 (November 1973): 1180–1184; see also Dr. I. Lee Coyne, "Exploring Sugar," accessed March 19, 2013, leanseekers.com/articles /health-issues/sugar.

24.   Nelson, *375 Meatless Recipes,* 136.

25.   White, *Counsels on Diet and Foods,* 327.

1958 Complete Health Program

We have just completed our *Natural Lifestyle Cooking* classes. I'm sure you are wondering, *How can I remember all the material presented in this class?* My husband always says, "When we come to the end of our classes, make sure it is simple enough for everyone to remember the important things." I would like to make it very simple for you. Just remember the 1958 program. Have you ever wished you could go back to the "good old days" of 1958? The prices of 1958 would sure seem great about now. The average cost of a new house was $12,750.00. The average monthly rent was $92.00. The cost of a gallon of gas was $0.25 and bread was only $0.19 a loaf. However, the average yearly salary was only about $4,600.00.

There were some **famous food innovations** in 1958. Some of you may even remember that Jif® Creamy Peanut Butter was introduced in stores for the first time. Others may remember that eighteen-year-old Frank Carney borrowed six hundred dollars from his mother to open the first Pizza Hut restaurant in Wichita, Kansas. This popular chain of restaurants is still going strong today. You may remember that the first potato flake manufacturing plant opened in Grand Forks, North Dakota. You may not recall everything that happened in 1958, but just remember that date because **the numbers will help you summarize several principles that are significant for good health.** Here it is:

1958

1 **SPEND ONE HOUR WITH GOD DAILY.** Medical research confirms the fact that religion has a positive correlation to our health. Our health actually improves when we trust in God's unconditional love. The Bible is full of encouraging promises. You may want to start reading the book of Proverbs in the Old Testament Scriptures. It has a lot of good wisdom for us. It presents practical, common sense principles on **how to be "healthy, wealthy, and wise."** It is a great place to start reading your Bible.

9 **EAT NINE FRUITS AND VEGETABLES EVERY DAY.** We are what we eat! God designed the Eden diet at Creation for our health. Start including more fruits and vegetables in your diet. The American Dietetic Association recommends that we eat nine fruits and vegetables daily. To enjoy the best health, eat a variety of these natural products of the earth. We can certainly improve our health significantly if we just incorporate this one principle of nutrition.

5 **WALK FIVE MILES A DAY FIVE TIMES A WEEK OUTSIDE IN THE FRESH AIR AND SUNSHINE.** Exercise is one of the Creator's important health principles. If we want to enjoy a happier, healthier, and longer life, we must keep moving. Numerous research studies today show that exercise is essential for good health. Typically, you will walk two miles just in your normal routine. This means that if you walk forty-five minutes to an hour a day extra, you will get your adequate exercise. Most everyone can at least walk daily. Walk with your head and shoulders erect, and it will do wonders for your health.

8 **DRINK EIGHT, 8-OUNCE GLASSES OF WATER DAILY.** Water is one of God's natural remedies for optimum health. It is essential to lubricate the system and keep it running smoothly. Our health depends on water. It is one of God's greatest blessings to our health.

GET EIGHT HOURS OF SLEEP A NIGHT. Sleep rejuvenates and rebuilds the body. It refreshes the mind and uplifts the spirit. Adequate rest enables us to function at optimum capacity.

AS AN ADDED BONUS, GIVE EIGHT HUGS A DAY TO SOMEONE. LOVE PEOPLE. Loving relationships are part of a healthy lifestyle. Love is a gift from God that is one of the most powerful and wonderful healing powers in the world.

So here you have it! All the **eight natural laws for good health are wrapped up in 1958.** As you incorporate these principles into your lifestyle, it will make a remarkable difference in your life. Our parting wish for you is that **you will follow these eight natural laws of health so you will be well, stay well, prosper, and be in health.**

Appendix

GROCERY LIST

Having a grocery shopping list can save you time, energy, and money.

Knowing exactly what you have on hand and the ingredients you need at the grocery store to feed your family healthy meals can be very helpful. Keep a list on your refrigerator so you don't forget those important items. Here is a sample of my list that I have just begun. My grandson, Dyson, will remind me if I missed any of his favorite foods and need to add them to my list, especially the ingredients for a fresh fruit strawberry smoothie. Following is a complete *Natural Lifestyle Cooking* shopping list to assist you in making the recipes in the cookbook.

seasons greetings

Grocery List

Whole wheat flour
Yeast
Quick oats
raisins
date
lentil
almonds
Corn meal

Natural Lifestyle Cooking Shopping List

BAKING SUPPLIES

- ☐ Baking powder, Rumford®
- ☐ Barley, pearl
- ☐ Barley flour
- ☐ Bran
- ☐ Brown sugar, light
- ☐ Bulgur wheat
- ☐ Coconut flakes
- ☐ Cornmeal, course ground
- ☐ Cornstarch
- ☐ Flaxseed, brown
- ☐ Flour, rye
- ☐ Flour, unbleached enriched white
- ☐ Flour, whole-wheat
- ☐ Flour, whole-wheat pastry
- ☐ Honey
- ☐ Maple syrup
- ☐ Molasses, Grandma's®
- ☐ Oats, quick, Quaker®
- ☐ Salt
- ☐ Vital wheat gluten flour
- ☐ Wheat berries
- ☐ Wheat germ

LEGUMES

- ☐ Beans, garbanzo beans, dried
- ☐ Beans, Great Northern, dried
- ☐ Beans, soy, dried
- ☐ Lentils
- ☐ Split peas

CANNED OR BOXED FOODS

- ☐ Applesauce, unsweetened
- ☐ Beans, chili
- ☐ Beans, garbanzo
- ☐ Beans, kidney
- ☐ Chinese noodles
- ☐ Corn flakes
- ☐ Fruit cocktail in fruit juice
- ☐ Italian dressing
- ☐ Mandarin oranges
- ☐ Mushrooms
- ☐ Pasta, mixed
- ☐ Pasta sauce, Prego®
- ☐ Pasta, spinach
- ☐ Peanut butter, Smucker's® natural chunky
- ☐ Pineapple juice, unsweetened
- ☐ Rice, brown, long grain
- ☐ Rice, brown, short grain
- ☐ Special K® cereal or equivalent
- ☐ Tomato paste
- ☐ Tomatoes, stewed
- ☐ Tomatoes, whole

SPECIALITY FOODS

- ☐ Big Franks
- ☐ Bragg® Liquid Aminos
- ☐ Breading meal, Cedar Lake®
- ☐ Brewer's yeast
- ☐ Carob
- ☐ Egg replacer
- ☐ Flaxseed
- ☐ George Washington's Seasoning and Broth
- ☐ McKay's® Chicken Style Instant Broth and Seasoning
- ☐ McKay's® Beef Style Instant Broth and Seasoning
- ☐ Soy flour
- ☐ Vegetarian burger

BREAD FOODS

- ☐ Bread crumbs
- ☐ Pita bread
- ☐ Stuffing mix

NUTS

- ☐ Almonds
- ☐ Almonds, slivered

- ☐ Cashews, raw
- ☐ Cashews, roasted
- ☐ Pecans
- ☐ Pine nuts
- ☐ Walnuts

DRIED FOODS
- ☐ Apricots, dried Turkish
- ☐ Dates
- ☐ Dates, Medjool
- ☐ Raisins

SEASONINGS
- ☐ Basil
- ☐ Bay leaf
- ☐ Caraway seeds
- ☐ Chives
- ☐ Coriander
- ☐ Cumin
- ☐ Garlic powder
- ☐ Italian seasoning
- ☐ Marjoram
- ☐ Olive oil, light
- ☐ Olive oil, regular
- ☐ Oregano
- ☐ Parsley
- ☐ Sage
- ☐ Sweet basil
- ☐ Turmeric
- ☐ Vanilla extract, McCormick®
- ☐ Vegetable bouillon cubes

REFRIGERATED ITEMS
- ☐ Earth Balance® spread
- ☐ Orange juice
- ☐ Soy mayonnaise
- ☐ Soymilk, Silk®
- ☐ Soy whipped cream
- ☐ Soy yogurt, Silk® strawberry
- ☐ Tofu, extra firm
- ☐ Tofu, firm or extra firm

FRESH FOODS
- ☐ Apples, Golden Delicious
- ☐ Avocados
- ☐ Bananas
- ☐ Blackberries
- ☐ Blueberries
- ☐ Cantaloupe
- ☐ Carrots
- ☐ Cauliflower
- ☐ Celery
- ☐ Eggplant
- ☐ Garlic
- ☐ Grapes
- ☐ Kiwi
- ☐ Lettuce, green leaf
- ☐ Lettuce, romaine
- ☐ Lime
- ☐ Mangoes
- ☐ Mint
- ☐ Mixed greens
- ☐ Onions
- ☐ Parsley
- ☐ Peaches
- ☐ Pepper, green bell
- ☐ Pepper, red bell
- ☐ Potatoes, sweet
- ☐ Potatoes, white
- ☐ Scallions
- ☐ Spinach
- ☐ Strawberries
- ☐ Tomatoes

FROZEN FOODS
- ☐ Blackberries
- ☐ Broccoli cuts
- ☐ Broccoli spears
- ☐ Mangoes
- ☐ Peaches
- ☐ Peas
- ☐ Pineapple
- ☐ Strawberries

Index

Notes